Martin Arz

IT'S SO MUNICH!

Your **KEY** to
MUNICH'S CENTRE
and the districts of
GLOCKENBACH
SCHWABING
HAIDHAUSEN
MAXVORSTADT
NEUHAUSEN · etc.

HIRSCHK FER
verlag

Contents

Moosach

90 BMW W

91 Olympiapark

89 Ost-West-Friedenskirc

81 Blutenburg

79 Hubertusbrunnen

80 Nymphenburg

78 Herz-Jesu-Kirche

Neuhausen

Friedenheim

Laim

Westend
Schwanthalerhöhe

77 Verkehrszentrum

75 Endlose Treppe

76 Sweet Brown Snail

38 St.

39 Theresienwies

40 Oktoberfest

74 Bavaria

72 Westpark

71 Sendlinger Mordweihnacht

35 A

37 Street-Art

73 Flaucher

Sendling

Sendling-
Westpark

Untersendling

Mittersendling

92 Versunkenes Dorf   93 Allianz Arena

Schwabing

Oberför

85 Münchner Freiheit

84 St. Ursula   88 St. Sylvester

87 Kleinhesseloher See

86 Suresnes

82 Elisabethmarkt

83 Walking Man

er Nordfriedhof   54 Academy of Fine Arts

53 Siegestor

47 TUM   50 Universität   30 Englischer Garten

48 Pinakotheken   51 St. Ludwig

52 Staatsbibliothek

46 Present
Continous   28 Haus der Kunst

29 Eisbachsurfer

55 Friedensengel

alast   41 Wittelsbacherbrunnen   31 Nationalmuseum   56 Villa Stuck

Kreuzviertel   27 St. Anna

Graggenau   57 Maximilianeum

32 St. Lukas   58 Wiener Platz

59 Herbergen

60 Müllersches
Volksbad

Detail
see next page   61 Gasteig

34 Gärtnerplatztheater

33 Deutsches Museum

36 St. Maximilian   62 French Quarter

64 Auer Dult

63 Kultfabrik   Berg am
Laim

68 Rosengarten

67 Little Venice

65 Feldmüllersiedlung

66 Heilig-Kreuz   Ramersdorf

Templer   70 Hellabrunn

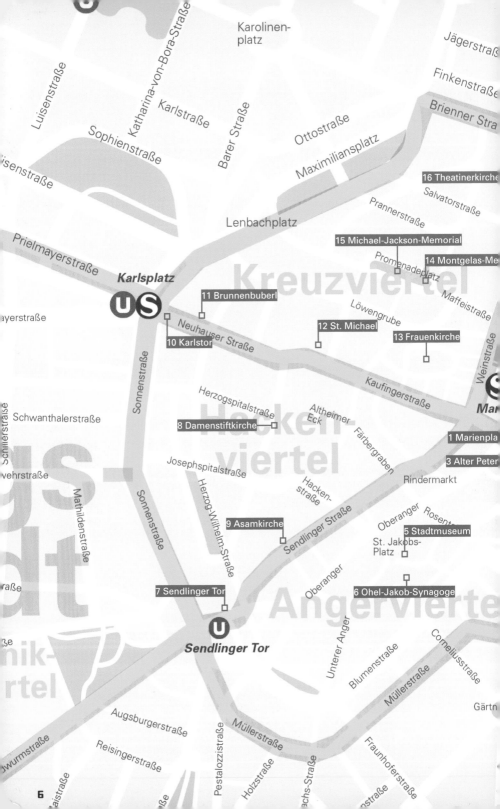

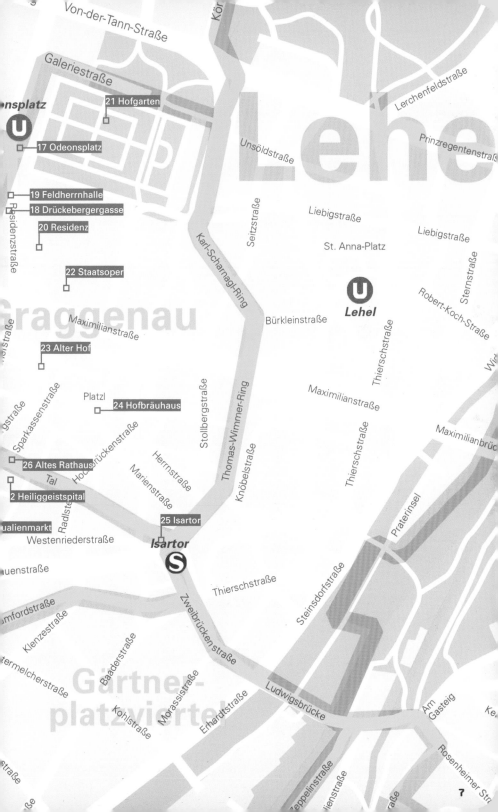

Von-der-Tann-Straße

Kör

Galeriestraße

Lerchenfeldstraße

onsplatz

U

21 Hofgarten

17 Odeonsplatz

Lehe

Prinzregen

Unsöldstraße

19 Feldherrnhalle

18 Drückebergergasse

sidenzstraße

Seitzstraße

Liebigstraße

Liebigstraße

20 Residenz

St. Anna-Platz

Sternstraße

22 Staatsoper

U

Lehel

Robert-Koch-Straße

Graggenau

Maximilianstraße

Bürkleinstraße

Thierschstraße

23 Alter Hof

Stollbergstraße

Maximilianstraße

Maximilianbrüc

Sparkassenstraße

Platzl

24 Hofbräuhaus

Thomas-Wimmer-Ring

Knöbelstraße

Thierschstraße

gstraße

Hochbrückenstraße

Herrnstraße

Marienstraße

Praterinsel

26 Altes Rathaus

Tal

2 Heiliggeistspital

Radlste

ualienmarkt

25 Isartor

Westenriederstraße

Isartor

S

Thierschstraße

Steinsdorfstraße

uenstraße

mfordstraße

Klenzestraße

Zweibrückenstraße

Am

Gasteig

Ke

termelcherstraße

Baaderstraße

Morassistraße

Gärtner-

platzviertel

Kohlstraße

Erhardtstraße

Ludwigsbrücke

Zeppelinstraße

ienstraße

Rosenheimer Str.

straße

Munich

As always, it was ultimately a matter of money and power. Heinrich der Löwe (Henry the Lion), Duke of Bavaria and Saxony, resented Bishop Otto of Freising for controlling the bridge across the river Isar and thus the profitable salt trade, which earned him good money through customs duties. For that reason, Heinrich had the bridge destroyed and his own bridge built just a short way further up the river where he set up customs facilities on top of a small hill nearby a monastery. Bishop Otto complained to Emperor Friedrich Barbarossa but the emperor ruled on 14th June 1158 that the new site »by the monks« was to benefit from market and customs rights. This was Munich's hour of birth. Munich developed rapidly and was therefore chosen by the Bavarian rulers from the House of Wittelsbach to become a royal seat. It was also capital of the Holy Roman Empire of German Nations during the 14th century under Emperor Ludwig the Bavarian. The city itself remained protected behind city walls until 1790 when the Elector Karl Theodor decided that Munich should no longer be a fort and had the city walls demolished and the moats filled in. The suburbs were born and then methodically developed around the Old Town. Munich grew and grew, swallowing up villages and even towns from surrounding areas. Now, Munich has long become a city with a population of over a million, making it a very expensive and wealthy place but also one of the Germany's safest cities.

Munich's centre

When people talk about an urban quarter these days it is often misleading as a city is normally divided into more than just four quarters. However, this is exactly the case for Munich's Old Town. The main circuit for residents and tourists is the *Neuhauser* and *Kaufingerstraße* where one can find many shops and places to eat and drink. For those who do not feel comfortable among masses of people, it is advisable to avoid Munich's Old Town particularly on Saturdays. The hustle and bustle continues at the *Marienplatz* and the *Wein-/Theatinerstraße*. Those who also want to appreciate the amenities of the city and do more than just shopping, can drift along the pedestrian zone, which was created in 1972 and glance into the many colourful shop windows. Needless to say, the Second World War and the post-war architecture have left severe traces on the cityscape. Then the »Second Destruction of Munich« followed in the 1960s where many historical buildings, which had survived the war but were considered as »old stuff«, fell victim to the wrecker's ball. The best example is the bunker-like department store *Kaufhof* at the *Marienplatz*. Its preceding building from the period of promoterism had survived the nightly bomb attacks during the war. Yet, some buildings were lovingly rebuilt after the war and that could be why the mix of styles from different eras creates this unique flair of the city centre since its formation. Moreover, as soon as the sun comes out people gets lured into the many cafés and restaurants with their outdoor areas. Then you realise why Munich is called »the northernmost city of Italy«.

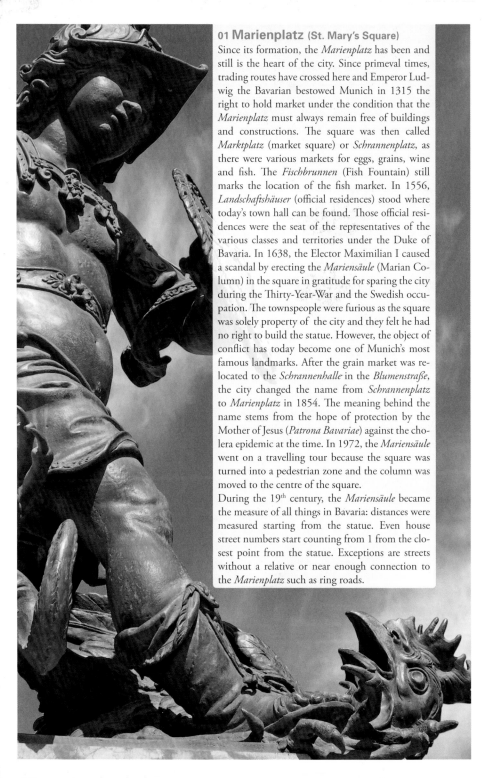

01 Marienplatz (St. Mary's Square)

Since its formation, the *Marienplatz* has been and still is the heart of the city. Since primeval times, trading routes have crossed here and Emperor Ludwig the Bavarian bestowed Munich in 1315 the right to hold market under the condition that the *Marienplatz* must always remain free of buildings and constructions. The square was then called *Marktplatz* (market square) or *Schrannenplatz*, as there were various markets for eggs, grains, wine and fish. The *Fischbrunnen* (Fish Fountain) still marks the location of the fish market. In 1556, *Landschaftshäuser* (official residences) stood where today's town hall can be found. Those official residences were the seat of the representatives of the various classes and territories under the Duke of Bavaria. In 1638, the Elector Maximilian I caused a scandal by erecting the *Mariensäule* (Marian Column) in the square in gratitude for sparing the city during the Thirty-Year-War and the Swedish occupation. The townspeople were furious as the square was solely property of the city and they felt he had no right to build the statue. However, the object of conflict has today become one of Munich's most famous landmarks. After the grain market was relocated to the *Schrannenhalle* in the *Blumenstraße*, the city changed the name from *Schrannenplatz* to *Marienplatz* in 1854. The meaning behind the name stems from the hope of protection by the Mother of Jesus (*Patrona Bavariae*) against the cholera epidemic at the time. In 1972, the *Mariensäule* went on a travelling tour because the square was turned into a pedestrian zone and the column was moved to the centre of the square.

During the 19th century, the *Mariensäule* became the measure of all things in Bavaria: distances were measured starting from the statue. Even house street numbers start counting from 1 from the closest point from the statue. Exceptions are streets without a relative or near enough connection to the *Marienplatz* such as ring roads.

Basics

Ultimately, the *Angerviertel* is Munich's core as this is the location of the *Petersbergl* (Peter's hill) and the church St. Peter that already existed long before the formation of Munich in 1158. The *Petersbergl* provided protection from the unpredictable river Isar and its dreaded floods. This was the reason why Duke Henry the Lion built his customs office on the hill right next to the small monastery. The district *Angerviertel* got its name from the surrounding grass and meadowland, which was mentioned first in 1300 and today makes up the area of the *St.-Jakobs-Platz* and *Sebastiansplatz*. Predominantly, the main inhabitants in the *Angerviertel* were traders, however, the hangman was located there too. His house was situated on the edge of the district where the main fire brigade is situated at the *Blumenstraße* today. Right next to the hangman's house, Munich's first brothel opened in November 1437 and was referred to at the time as *Frauenhaus* (women's house). The brothel's neighbour, the hangman, also acted as the official brothel keeper as well as pimp, paid by the city authorities. During the first half of the 13th century, the brothers of the Franciscan Order settled down by the *Anger*. A small hermitage including the *Jakobskapelle* (Chapel of St. Jacob) has been there for many cen-

existence. The vibrating and colourful centre of the Angerviertel is the *Viktualienmarkt* (food market), which is Germany's largest outdoor food market.

Munich's centre: **Angerviertel**

First mentioned 15th September 1508 as »Anngerfiertl« **Meaning** »Anger« = grass or meadowland **Location** south east of the Old Town, between Tal, Marienplatz, Sendlinger Straße and Müllerstraße

turies, which attracted pilgrims who were passing through towards the Alps. The Franciscan Order moved into the newly built monastery *St. Anton*, near the Imperial Residence in 1284 at the request of Duke Ludwig der Strenge (Louis the Strict). In the same year, nuns of the Order of St. Clare took over the convent *St. Jakob*, which quickly rose to become one of the most significant and wealthy convents. At the end of the 18th century, the convent introduced a school for girls. Since 1843, the congregation of the School Sisters of Notre Dame resides at Munich's oldest convent. Opposite the convent is Munich's new Jewish Centre along with the main synagogue *Ohel Jakob* (Jacob's Tent), the community centre as well as the Jewish Museum. Finally, you can also find the *Münchner Stadtmuseum* (City Museum of Munich) at the *St.-Jakobs-Platz*. Naturally, where there was a trading quarter, markets nearby were not hard to find. Only bronze statues of cows at the cattle market (*Rindermarkt*) remind us today of its

Jedes
Menschen
leben
soll heilig
sein
Kurt Eisner

13

02 Heiliggeistspital (Hospice of the Holy Spirit)

Originally, just a small romanesque chapel that formed part of a hospice which was set up in 1208. The hospice and chapel were destroyed during the great fire in the city in 1327. A new and bigger gothic church was built and completed in 1392. In order to keep up with the architectural progress, the hospice was then redesigned in the baroque style in the 18ᵗʰ century only to be demolished in 1806 to make way for the *Viktualienmarkt*. At the end of the 19ᵗʰ century, the nave of the church was extended by 3 acres westwards and completed the construction with a neo-baroque façade. Viktualienmarkt 1 • **U/S** Marienplatz

03 Alter Peter (St. Peter's Church)

Popularly called »Old Peter«, it is the oldest church within the historic city centre of Munich. Monks from the monastery Tegernsee already founded a settlement including a chapel on top of Peter's hill during the 8th century. The site had already been colonised for a while, as data shows. A new construction in gothic style was consecrated in 1294, which replaced the small romanesque chapel. »Old Peter« was, like many other churches, redeveloped in the 17th century to match the new baroque style. The relics of a Christian martyr can still be found inside the »Old Peter«. Precious gold embroidery and jewels enshroud the remains of St. Munditia. Rindermarkt 1 • U/S Marienplatz

04 Viktualienmarkt

One can hardly believe it but in its place stood once the hospice *Heiliggeistspital* and the rest of the area was a marshland with numerous streams flowing through the city of Munich. Until the hospice was eventually demolished and the streams drained to construct the market on its grounds instead, since the usual market square *Marienplatz* was bursting at the seams at the beginning of the 19th century. There are no streams anymore and the *Viktualienmarkt* with its abundant offerings and the centrally located beer garden has become a favourite spot among the residents and tourists. The city council made one of its smarter decisions after the Second World War when it originally planned to relocate the heavily destroyed *Viktualienmarkt* and use the space to construct high-rise buildings instead. Even the urban motorway was to run directly next to the market but eventually it was decided to save Munich's landmark.

There has not been great success in integrating the new *Schrannenhalle*, a smaller version of the once enormous *Schrannenhalle* that sprawled along the *Blumenstraße* from 1850. **U/S** Marienplatz

05 Münchner Stadtmuseum (City Museum of Munich)

The *Museum der Stadt München* (City Museum of Munich) is set within a medieval backdrop. The oldest building, the *Zeughaus* (armoury) derives from the year 1500 and formed together with the adjoining *Marstall* (stable and riding school) and other buildings the city museum in 1888. Today it is Germany's largest communal museum. The permanent exhibition »*Typisch München*« (Typically Munich) shows documents and objects about the city's history. Another permanent exhibition is »*Chiffren der Erinnerung*« about the National Socialism movement in Munich. Moreover, there are photo exhibitions, musical instruments, contemporary history as well as a puppet theatre and fairground attractions. Movie lovers get their fix at the film museum with its daily changing programme. St.-Jakobs-Platz 1 • U Sendlinger Tor • tue–sun: 10.00–18.00

06 Ohel-Jakob-Synagoge

Germany's second largest Jewish community has a hub again in Munich's centre since 2006. The architects Wandel, Hoefer and Lorch from Saarbrücken designed the Jewish communal centre and the 28m high Ohel Jakob synagogue, whose stone plinth is evocative of the Wailing Wall in Jerusalem. The grounds were provided for free by the city of Munich. 4500 names of Jewish residents, who were killed during the Nazi regime, are eternalised throughout a 32m long underground tunnel called *»Gang der Erinnerung«* (Walk of Remembrance) connecting the buildings.

St.-Jakobs-Platz 16 • **U/S** Marienplatz

Basics

»Where Munich is truly Munich« – that is the slogan of the shops in the district *Hackenviertel*. In fact, the *Hackenviertel* breaks the mould slightly compared to the rest of the Old Town. You can hardly find any prestigious constructions or famous sights here. The district has always been the home of tradesmen and grocers. However, the history of the *Hackenviertel* is considerably older then Munich's because there once was a small village, whose history is unknown apart from the fact that it existed long before the formation of Munich. It featured a small castle called *Altheim*. Duke Albrecht III erected a small chapel in *Altheim* in 1440 the former building of today's *Damenstifts-kirche* (Church of St. Anna). The village of *Altheim* was simply swallowed up during an extension of the city and integrated in its city walls.

The *Hackenviertel* and the *Angerviertel*, then and just like today divided by the *Sendlinger Straße*, belonged during the Middle Ages to the parish of *St. Peter*. The appending cemetery was situated in the *Hacken-viertel* from 1478 of which only the former cemetery chapel, the *Kreuzkirche*, remains today. Few tourists stray to the church. The more photogenic and pre-stigious sight is the *Asamkirche* (Asam Church) in the *Sendlinger Straße*, which is a masterpiece of the

Munich's centre: Hackenviertel

First mentioned 29th December 1458 as »Hagken vierteil« **Meaning** »Hacken« (Hag, Hagen, Gehag) = enclosed property/estate **Location** south west of the Old Town bet-ween Sendlinger-, Rosen-, Kaufinger-, Neuhau-ser Straße and Sonnenstraße

late baroque era. Also, from the late baroque era is the *Damenstiftskirche*, which looks rather plain from the outside. Even more unimpressive on the outside is the former hospice *Herzogspital* and the church *Herzogspitalkirche St. Elisabeth* within its courtyard. The site was heavily damaged during the war and replaced by a clinker construction in the 1950s, housing the convent of the Order of the Servite Sisters. In contrast, one of the oldest and still existing community centres in Munich as well as the oldest pub from 1440 – the *Gasthaus zur Hundskugel* in the *Hotterstraße* – largely survived the centuries intact. A new luxurious residential and commercial develop-ment, called *Hofstatt,* was created adjacent to these buildings. This was not the first intervention with the old structure as during the 1980s, the old back-yard workshops next to the *Asamkirche* were torn down and the new housing complex *Asamhof* was built instead.

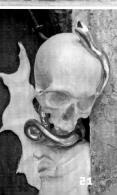

07 Sendlinger Tor (Sendling Gate)

The *Sendlinger Tor* was created when Emperor Ludwig the Bavarian extended the city and raised a new town fortification between 1285 and 1337. The gate was first mentioned in 1318 when it was marked as the starting point for the route to Italy. The central tower was demolished in 1808. Due to traffic issues, a single large arch replaced the three arches that connected the two outer towers in 1906. **U** Sendlinger Tor

08 Damenstiftskirche (Church of St. Anna)

The ceiling fresco is black and white! Unusual for a baroque church but this is due to the destruction of the church during the Second World War. At the time of the restoration, only black and white photographs existed of the frescos by the brothers Asam. To avoid using the wrong colours the restorers only used black and white paint. The church dates back to a chapel, which was erected by Duke Albrecht III in 1440 in the village of *Altheim* outside the gates of Munich. After Munich incorporated *Altheim*, Elector Karl Albrecht, who later became Emperor Karl VII, built a new church in 1733 for the Order of the Salesian Sisters. The former convent next to the church is now a Secondary School. Damenstiftstraße1-3 • U/S Karlstor

09 Asamkirche (Asam Church)

Two genius brothers created a masterpiece of the late baroque era but only for themselves. The painter and architect Cosmas Damian Asam and the plasterer and sculptor Egid Quirin Asam built their personal and private church right next Egid Quirin's house in the *Sendlinger Straße*. Because they had no employer as such, they were able to work free to their own imagination. The small but spectacular church emerged between 1733 and 1746 with its official name *St.-Johann-Nepomuk* but everyone in Munich calls it *Asamkirche*. Egid Quirin Asam had a window assembled in his house that enabled him direct views on to the altar of the church. However, due to protests of the townspeople the brothers Asam were forced to open »their« church to the public. Sendlinger Straße 62 • **U** Sendlinger Tor

Basics

The wealthy history of the district *Kreuzviertel* remains still unnoticed today. During the Middle Ages, this was the site of the *Salzstadel* (salt warehouse), which stored the salt to which Munich owed his wealth and existence. Right here in this spot the world-famous landmark of Munich was built: the *Frauenkirche* (Cathedral of Our Dear Lady). Wealthy merchants and Patricians settled down around the church and the salt warehouse. The powerful society and the clergy discovered the district towards the end of the 16th century. Duke Wilhelm V had 54 townhouses demolished and the prestigious *Palace Maxburg* constructed on the edge of the district. The palace was destroyed during the war and replaced in the 1950s by a controversial complex called *Neue Maxburg*. Only the renaissance tower remains. Construction of the extensive Jesuit convent with the Old Academy and the *Michaelskirche* started at the same time. Eventually, the Carmelite Order also settled down there and the Capuchin Order built a monastery outside the city walls. The *Kreuzviertel* established itself finally as Munich's clerical centre with the erection of the church *Theatinerkirche*. Since 1818, the archbishop of Munich and Freising also resides in the *Palais Holnstein* in the *Kardinal-*gious office buildings. In the 19th century other palaces had to make way to the new power-domiciles of the modern era, such as the banks. The *Hypo-Vereinsbank* is represented with multiple buildings in the neo-baroque style. The bank also had one of the blocks of buildings stripped out during the turn of the millennium in order to develop the exclusive shopping arcade *5 Höfe* and the *Hypo-Kunsthalle*. This passage now connects the financial district with the shopping mall in the *Theatinerstraße*.

Munich's centre: Kreuzviertel

First mentioned 29th December 1458 as »Kreutz vierteil« **Meaning** named after the passageway Kreuzgasse, today the Promenadeplatz and Pacellistraße **Location** north west of the Old Town between Neuhauser-, Kaufingerstraße, Marienplatz, Wein-, Theatinerstraße and Altstadtring

Faulhaber-Straße. More and more aristocrats started to set up their homes in the *Kreuzviertel* in the 17th century, particularly along the *Prannerstraße* and the *Promenadeplatz*, e.g. the families of the Porcias, Preysings, Montgelas, Spretis, Toerring-Jettenbachs and many more. Governmental departments moved into the district in the 19th century. The State Parliament held meetings in the *Prannerstraße*, the Ministry of the Interior occupied the rooms of the former convent *Theatinerkloster* and the Foreign Secretary, simultaneously chairman of the Council of Ministers and virtually Prime Minister, resided in the *Palais Montgelas*. The latter is today part of the *Hotel Bayerischer Hof*.

Many of the baroque and rococo styled, old aristocratic palaces are still preserved today and create the unique charm of this district. Admittedly, they are not used as private residences anymore but presti-

GASSENSCHENKE

COMERCIAL

10 Karlstor (Karl's Gate)

The gate harboured a secret that was only lifted by accident during the building of the Stachus-Shopping centre in 1970. A secret tunnel made from brick stone was found which soldiers had used during an occupation to get from the *Karlstor* up to and behind the enemies lines. The *Karlstor* was mentioned for the first time in 1302 and was then called *Neuhauser Tor* because one left the city from here towards the district of Neuhausen. It was renamed *Karlstor* during renovation work in 1791 after the then reigning Elector Karl Theodor. The main tower in the centre was damaged so badly by an explosion in 1857 that it had to be torn down entirely. Arnold Zenetti redesigned the *Karlstor* in the neo-gothic style four years later. The subsequent *Stachus-Rondell* (Stachus crescent) by Gabriel von Seidl emerged between 1899 and 1902.

Incidentally, the people of Munich only call the *Karlsplatz* »*Stachus*«. The name relates to a pub, which was located just outside the gate (today the department store *Kaufhof*) and run by the landlord Eustachius Föderl in the 18th century. Eustachius' nickname was *Stachus* after which people started to call the pub *Stachus*. The square was also then renamed *Stachus*.

U/S Karlsplatz

11 Brunnenbuberl (Fountain Boy)

A naked child covers the water tap of the fountain with its hands to avoid the jet of water, in vain, because a cheeky satyr spits the water right down on to him. The sculptor Matthias Gasteiger created the fountain in 1895 and Prince Regent Luitpold himself asked the artist to cover the boy's modesty with a fig leave. Gasteiger refused and succeeded because art was unreserved in Munich at the time and overruled even royal requests. The fountain was originally located within a green space at the *Sonnenstraße* and was moved to its present location in 1971. Karlstor • **U/S** Karlstor

12 Michaelskirche (St. Michael's Church)

It was once referred to as the Eighth Wonder of the World! The *Michaelskirche*, built between 1583 and 1597, features the second largest barrel-vault in the world after the St. Peter's Basilica in Rome. Nobody expected this daring construction to survive but the roof lasted. The steeple however already crashed during its construction in 1590 and it was decided to omit the spire altogether. Stylistically, the church was modelled to the Church of the Gesù in Rome (Mother Church of the Society of Jesus). It was the first renaissance cathedral north of the Alps and became the role model for over 100 other church constructions. The facade is decorated with statues of various Bavarian rulers. Numerous Bavarian regents are buried in the royal tomb of St. Michael among them the »Swan King« Ludwig II. Neuhauser Straße 52 • **U/S** Karlsplatz

13 Frauenkirche (Cathedral of Our Dear Lady)

The small picture of the *Frauenkirche* on the right is a technical sensation. It is the first photograph to ever be taken in Germany. Carl August von Steinheil and Franz von Kobell invented a photographic process in 1839 and what else is there to photograph than the *Frauenkirche*? The Cathedral of Our Dear Lady, which is its official name, was the second parish church in Munich. Master builder Jörg Ganghofer built the present construction in only twenty years: a miracle in those days for such an enormous development. The cathedral was consecrated in 1494. Since 1525, the so-called *Welschen-Hauben* (onion-shaped domes), rest on top of the towers. The towers are 100m high and visible from afar as city administration prohibits any construction to stand taller than the towers of the cathedral within the ring road *Mittlerer Ring*.

Frauenplatz • U/S Marienplatz

14 Montgelas-Memorial

Maximilian Carl Joseph Franz de Paula Hieronymus Earl of Montgelas (1759–1838) served as minister under Max I and is considered to be the great Reformer of the State Bavaria. He rigorously executed the secularisation to disempower and dispossess the church and enforced the equality of the Christian Denominations. Montgelas modernised and reformed the administration, the finance and fiscal system and the legal system entirely. Karin Sander created the aluminium statue in 2005.

Promenadeplatz • **U/S** Karlsplatz

15 Orlando di Lasso-/Michael Jackson-Memorial

What does the most famous composer of the renaissance and the King of Pop have in common? Almost nothing except for the fact that they share the space of a monument in Munich. Orlando di Lasso (or Roland de Lassu, 1532–1594), born in the Netherlands, lived and worked in Munich from 1556. His last profession was court bandmaster. A monument was set up in his honour at the *Promenadeplatz*. Michael Jackson (1958–2009), pop star from the United States, stayed numerous times at the *Hotel Bayerischer Hof* across the road. That was reason enough for his fans to build a shrine after his death. The statue of di Lasso was the elected place for this shrine. Promenadeplatz • **U/S** Karlsplatz

16 Theatinerkirche (Theatine Church of St. Cajetan)

Electoral Princess Henriette Adelheid of Savoyen was delighted about the birth of an heir to the throne just as much as her husband Ferdinand Maria of Bavaria. Both expressed their joy in the form of monuments. Ferdinand Maria gave his wife the *Palace Nymphenburg* as a gift and in gratitude for giving birth to Max Emanuel. Henriette Adelheid made a gift to the city of Munich in the form of the *Theatinerkirche*. The work on the church in Italian late-baroque style started in 1663 opposite the Residence Palace. The church was to be royal church but also collegiate church for the Order of the Theatines. After the master builder Augusto Barelli had walked away after a dispute and left only the building shell, Enrico Zuccalli took on the exterior design of the church. François de Cuvilliés Snr. produced the current façade in 1765. Noticeable on the inside of the church is the rich white stucco, which is usually painted in vivid colours. The *Theatinerkirche* is burial plot to the Bavarian rulers such as Emperor Charles IV and King Max I Joseph.

Theatinerstraße 22 • **U** Odeonsplatz

Basics

Mainly Bavarian rulers left their mark in the *Graggenau* district. This was the seat of the representative and administrative offices such as the *Marstall* (stable and riding school) and the royal mint yard. The Old Court, which dates back to the 12th century, was Imperial Residence to the royal houses. Emperor Ludwig the Bavarian even appointed the castle to become Germany's first permanent Imperial Residence. The Imperial Regalia were kept in the chapel of the castle. In 1385, the monarchs built the present residence *Neuveste* as a refuge to be able to escape from the revolting citizens of Munich. The Wittelsbach family had the Residence continuously re-designed and extended by the best architects during the following centuries until they finally owned the largest municipal palace in Germany.

Rich Patrician families in Munich positioned their glamorous palaces near the Residence Palace. King Max I Joseph had his court and national theatre built in the place where, until the secularisation, a Franciscan monastery and pastoral centre of the *Graggenau* was situated. Max II, the grandson of Max I, put a further stamp on to the *Graggenau* district: the *Maximilianstraße*. Taunted as a total failure by people at the time, the boulevard is today one of Germany's

ched one of Einbeck's best master brewers to quench the thirst for beer in Munich's court.

Not only were royal powers represented in the *Graggenau* but also civic administration offices. The Old and the New Town Hall both are situated here whereas many tourists mistake the New Town Hall for the old one. Numerous private townhouses had to be demolished at the end of the 19th century on the northern side of the *Marienplatz* to make space for the neo-gothic New Town Hall. The small green oasis called *Marienhof* can be found right here in the centre and to the north of the town hall. The area was originally occupied by buildings but was destroyed by bombs during the Second World War.

Munich's centre: Graggenau

First mentioned 29th December 1458 as »Gragkenaw viertail« **Meaning** from »Gragg« or »Krack« = raven, crow and »Au« = floodplain (crow-floodplain) **Location** north east of the Old Town between Theatiner-, Weinstraße, Marienplatz, Tal and Altstadtring

finest shopping avenues. Ludwig I, father of Max II, apparently screamed »disgusting, disgusting, disgusting« when he saw it.

The *Graggenau* only presented itself magnificently upstream from the ledge of the river Isar. Craftsmen mainly settled down in the valley as the hydrodynamic power of the city streams provided the necessary energy for many businesses. Until today, the only active flourmill in Munich remains in the *Neuturmstraße 3*, called the *Hofbräuhaus-Kunstmühle*. The medieval characteristics of the area are still visible in the *Graggenau* through the entwined and narrow passages. The centre of the lower *Graggenau* is the square *Platzl* with the *Hofbräuhaus* (Royal Brewery), which was founded in 1607 by Duke Wilhelm V who enjoyed well-brewed beer and had to import it from Einbeck near Hanover because the beer in Munich tasted so poor at the time. In order to save on the high transport costs the Duke poa-

17 Odeonsplatz

He hated Munich. Crown Prince Ludwig, who later became King Ludwig I had wanted to leave Munich. Therefore, his father King Max I decided that his son had to be distracted and gave him free reign to design the borough *Max-vorstadt*. Ludwig decided »I want to turn Munich into the city that defines Germany and everyone who travels though the country will only get to know the land if they come through Munich«. The former city walls had consistently been broken down since 1791 and the old *Schwabinger Tor* had to give way as well. Ludwig I commissioned the architect Leo von Klenze with the design of his dream of the »*Isar-Athen*«. Klenze had the gate demolished and the grounds levelled to create an enormous square, which was to provide the new and magnificent boulevard *Ludwigstraße*. Klenze built around the square in the 1820s to create the concert hall *Odeon* (today the Ministry of the Interior), the *Leuchtenberg Palace* (today the Treasury) and the bazaar building, which still contains Munich's oldest coffee house *Tambosi*, formed in 1774. The *Odeonsplatz* by the way was just a field of debris after the war. The palaces and the bazaar building are replicas but true to their originals. U Odeonsplatz

18 Drückebergergasse

On 9th November 1923, outside the *Feldherrnhalle* (Field Marshals' Hall), Hitler failed to seize power in Munich with the so-called Munich Putsch (Beer Hall Putsch). Four policeman and 16 rebels died during the putsch. In 1933, a memorial was installed for the dead revolutionists on the eastern side of the *Feldherrnhalle* with the inscription »And you triumphed nevertheless!«. A SS guard of honour watched over the monument. Everyone who passed by had to mark their respect with the Nazi salute. Those who wanted to avoid such gesture chose the path through the small passageway *Viscardigasse* towards the *Theatinerstraße* and the *Feldhernhalle*. Ever since that time the people of Munich call the small alley *Drückebergergasse* (shirker alley). In 1995, as a reminder to the civilian resistance, sculptor Bruno Wank created an S-shaped, curved track made from bronze and recessed into the cobblestones of the *Viscardigasse*. Viscadrigasse • U Odeonsplatz

19 Feldherrnhalle (Field Marshals' Hall)

Unmistakeably, the Loggia dei Lanzi of Florence was the inspiration for the *Feldherrnhalle*. Friedrich von Gärtner designed the loggia after its Italian model between 1841 and 1844 as opening to the *Odeonsplatz* and *Ludwigstraße*. The *Schwabinger Tor*, which stood in its former place, was demolished and the city walls levelled. The loggia is dedicated to the Bavarian army and is twinned with the *Siegestor*, which is one kilometre away. The *Feldherrnhalle* was to be the new viewpoint after the demolition of the *Schwabinger Tor*. Ludwig von Schwanthaler designed the bronze statues of Earl Tilly and Prince Wrede. The Bavarian Army monument in its centre is a reminder of the victorious alliance with Bavaria during the Franco-Prussian war in 1870/71. Odeonsplatz • U Odeonsplatz

20 Residenz (Residence Palace)

After violent riots, the monarchs of Bavaria constructed a refuge including moats in 1385 on the edge of the city to barricade themselves against rebellious townsmen. During the centuries this palace became the Royal Palace of the Bavarian dukes, electors and kings. The rulers redesigned and extended the Residence Palace until it sprawled more and more into the city. An enormous complex developed with ten courtyards, the largest inner-city palace in Germany. The Residence invites you to a journey through time and centuries: all the essential European stylistic eras from gothic to renaissance, baroque to rococo up to classicism are represented. Parts of the Residence were open to interested citizens for viewings under King Ludwig I but only when the royal couple were absent. Until its destruction in the Second World War, the Residence had been the largest ambient art museum in the world. More than over 100 opulent rooms, apartments and ballrooms are open to the public today. Among them the Hall of Antiquities which Duke Albrecht V built between 1568 and 1571 for his collection of antique sculptures (see photo above). It is the oldest remaining room inside the Residence Palace and also the largest Renaissance hall north of the Alps. All the treasures accumulated by the Bavarian monarchs made up from gemstones, ivory and precious metals can be admired in the treasure chamber. Do not forget to rub the nose of one of the bronze lions that guard the entrance to the *Kaiserhof*; it is meant to bring luck! Residenzstraße 1 • U/S Odeonsplatz or Marienplatz • summer: 9.00–18.00, winter: 10.00–17.00

21 Hofgarten (Court Garden)

Argentine Tango, Salsa and Swing – lively dancing takes place in the middle of the garden because the *Dianatempel* (Diana's temple) is the meeting point for dance enthusiasts from all over Munich. The *Dianatempel* was created by Heinrich Schön Snr. in 1615 and is the centrepiece of the Court Gardens. Elector Maximilian I had the garden laid out in 1613-1617 in the Italian style of a renaissance garden. The Bavaria statue on top of the temple, casted by Hubert Gerhard in 1623, is merely a copy. The original can be found in the *Kaisersaal* (Imperial Hall) of the Residence Palace. From July to November 1937, the northern arcades of the Court Garden were the venue for one of the lowest points in German cultural history: a propaganda exhibition organised by the Nazis called »Degenerated Art«. A memorial at the entrance of the arcades to the Bavarian State Chancellery reminds since 1996 of the resistance against the Nazi dictatorship. **U/S** Odeonsplatz

22 Staatsoper (State Opera)

The opera was on fire! The set had caught fire during a performance on the 14th January 1823. All water sources were frozen due to the freezing night temperatures. As a result, King Max I had beer barrels from the *Hofbräuhaus* confiscated and poured on to the fire but to no avail. The new royal court and national theatre, opened on 12th October 1818 and designed by the architect Karl von Fischer, burned down. The reconstruction was completed in 1825. Two technical wonders made the theatre one of the most modern stages of the late 19th century: The first German theatre to receive electric lighting in 1883 and in 1896 the first revolving stage in the western world was activated during a production of Mozart's »Don Giovanni«. Many premieres of Richard Wagner's operas were held here under King Ludwig II. Nothing remained of the opera due to the nightly bombs of the Second World War. It was decided to rebuild the old theatre instead of building a new one. The reopening was celebrated in 1963. The Munich State Opera possesses, after Paris and Warsaw, the third largest opera stage in the world. Max-Joseph-Platz 2 • U/S Marienplatz

23 Alter Hof (Old Court)

The small child who one-day would become German Emperor, Ludwig the Bavarian, laid innocently in his cot when the tame house monkey came and took the baby out to play. The nursemaid cried out when she noticed it and the monkey got scared and ran with the baby under its arm across the castle to climb up to the top of the tower. The monkey returned the baby unharmed after some friendly persuasion. A lovely and very popular story: King Kong in Munich – with one small mistake: the small wooden tower was only built in 1470 and Emperor Ludwig the Bavarian died already in 1347…

The history of the Old Court dates back to the 12th century. The Bavarian monarchs ruled here from 1255. Emperor Ludwig the Bavarian declared the castle to be the first permanent Imperial Residence in Germany. In 1385, monarchs built a refuge on the grounds of the Residence to guard themselves from rebelling citizens. This refuge was extended and declared a seat of government. This led to the Old Court being left abandoned. Alter Hof • U/S Marienplatz

24 Hofbräuhaus (Royal Brewery)

Bavarian monarchs sourced their beer supplies from the hanseatic city of Einbeck near Hanover. In order to save money, Duke Wilhem V eventually decided to build the Royal Brewery in 1589 for personal use. However, the taste of the beer was not equal to the beer from Einbeck. Thus, Einbeck's best master brewer was lured away from the Prussians and Elias Pichler came into royal service in Bavaria in 1614 and brewed beer at the Royal Brewery according to »Einbecker« customs. Lazy pronunciation created the name »Ainpockbier« and eventually it became »Bock« beer. That is how »Bock« beer found its way to Munich. The *Hofbräuhaus* at the *Platzl* was already a major tourist attraction in 1896 so that the brewery had to be relocated to Haidhausen and the restaurant extended. Architect Max Littmann designed the new and current *Hofbräuhaus*, which opened its doors on 22nd September 1897. Platzl 9 • **U/S** Marienplatz • daily 09.00–23.30

25 Isartor (Isar Gate)

The *Isartor* is the best-preserved gate today. Unlike the others, the *Isartor* still features its main central tower, which is approximately 40m high as well as both towers on each side. It was built in 1337 as part of the major city extension under Emperor Ludwig the Bavarian. Those who travelled along the salt route entered the city through this gate. The city council intended to have the gate demolished in the early 19th century. However, King Ludwig I decided against it. He commissioned the architect Friedrich von Gärtner with the reconstruction according to its historic model. Bernhard von Neher painted the monolithic fresco above the three central arches as part of the renovation. It shows the victorious procession of Emperor Ludwig the Bavarian after the battle of Ampfing in 1322. The museum *Valentin-Karlstadt Musäum* (Karl Valentin and Liesl Karlstadt were extremely popular Munich comedians) is situated at the Isartor since 1959. The main tower on the western side was equipped with a clock in 2005. It runs anti-clockwise but thanks to its mirror-inverted dial it still displays the correct time. True to the Bavarian expression: »The clocks work differently in Bavaria.« Isartorplatz • **S** Isartor

26 Altes Rathaus (Old Town Hall)

Nobody knows what the first town hall in Munich looked like. It fell victim to a flash of lightning. Dome master builder Jörg Ganghofer, who also constructed the *Frauenkirche* at the same time, erected the gothic town hall between 1470 and 1480. Conveniently, the municipal prison was set up in the basement. A large ball and dance room was situated on the first floor and is still used for official functions today. Most parts of the ballroom are still in its original condition even though the building underwent several redesigns during the centuries. The famous *Moriskentänzer* (Morris dancers), hand carved by Erasmus Grasser in the 15th century, can be found in the ballroom. They are the world's only three-dimensional displays of the then popular dance style. However, these are copies and the originals are displayed in the City Museum of Munich. The passage routes to the *Tal* are fairly new as they were only built after the relocation of the city council to the New Town Hall in 1874. Today, the Toy Museum is also located in the tower of the Old Town Hall. Marienplatz 15 • **U/S** Marienplatz

Basics

No medieval city finished at the city walls. The so-called *Burgfrieden*, an area outside the castle walls, also belonged to the city. Parts of Munich's urban areas have always been the districts *Lehel, Gasteig, Isarvorstadt, Ludwigsvorstadt* and *Maxvorstadt*. Naturally, life outside the protective city walls was not easy. For one, there was the torrent river Isar with its dreaded floods and the barren soil of the forests called *Auwälder* provided no farming opportunities. On top of that, whoever occupied Munich during a war, ravaged the unguarded suburbs. The district *Lehel* was always ransacked by marauding troops. The residents of the *Lehel* had to endure the disasters patiently. Those who settled down there belonged to the lower class and had to survive as day labourer or follow a trade. Already in the dim and distant past, a blacksmith operated a smithy with a melting furnace in the *Lehel* according to findings from the Bronze Age. Waterpower provided the most important source of energy during the pre-industrial period. Numerous flourmills were set up along the backwaters of the river Isar. But not only flourmills profited from the power of the water. The wheels also powered mills for wood, stone, paper, cement and spices as well as the blacksmith's hammer. Addi-

The rafts were taken apart and the tree trunks were used as timber. The end of the harbour came when the railway became the more economical means of transportation. In order to replace the two inner-city ports the city built a central landing at *Maria Einsiedel* used only today for excursion boats.

The *Lehel* constantly attracted people seeking work with its harbour and industrial areas. Just like the workers living quarters in the districts *Au* and *Haidhausen*, the *Lehel* was hopelessly overcrowded. Every filthy chamber and dirty hole found a grateful lodger but what was missing was a church. On 19th May 1727, Electoral Princess Marie-Amalie laid the cornerstone for the convent *St. Anna*, which has since then been the heart of the district. The *Lehel* officially became *St.-Anna-Vorstadt* in 1814 after Munich tore down its city walls. However, the name never stuck. Slowly the quarter became trendy. King Maximillian II commissioned architect Friedrich Bürklein to construct a new boulevard from the *Max-Josephs-Platz* straight down to the river Isar. The *Maximiliamstraße*, completed in 1853 in the neo-gothic Tudor style, is today one of Germany's most exclusive shopping areas. The *Maximilianstraße* and the second boulevard *Prinzregentenstraße* enhanced the

Munich's centre: **Lehel**

First mentioned 1525 as »auf den lehen«
Meaning either from »Lehen« (= rights over land and property), or from »Lohe« (= small forest); since 1641 the lower Lehel, which forms the present area of the Lehel was divided from the upper Lehel, which forms todays district Isarvorstadt

tionally, launderers and tanners settled down by the water as well as the textile industry. A large cotton factory and three tobacco factories provided work for hundreds of the residents from the *Lehel*. One of the tobacco factories belonged to Pietro Paolo de Maffei from Verona, whose son Joseph Anton de Maffei set up a locomotive factory at the English Garden, which later became the industrial enterprise Krauss-Maffei.

The biggest economic factor in the *Lehel* however, was the raft port at the bridge *Ludwigsbrücke*. Munich maintained two raft ports at the time: one between the *Kohleninsel* (today *Museumsinsel*) and *Lehel* as well as between the *Westermühlbach* and the district *Isarvorstadt*. Munich possessed Europe's largest raft harbour in middle of the 19th century. Rafts from the foothills of the Alps landed here delivering goods from Italy and other parts of the Alps.

status of the *Lehel* immensely. The *Lehel* became middle-class. The influx of new residents remained unbroken. Many of the new citizens were Jewish and came from the Eastern part. They built the *Ohel-Jakob* synagogue in 1882 in the *Herzog-Rudolf-Straße*. The synagogue burned down during the massacres of the *Reichskristallnacht* (Night of Broken Glass) in 1938. Speaking of massacre: one person who knew the *Lehel* very well was Adolf Hitler as he used to live in the *Thierschstraße* for almost ten years. Hitler also set up the neo-classical *Haus der Kunst* (House of Art) in the *Lehel*. The bombs – the result of Hitler's delusion of the »Thousand Year Empire« – left the *Lehel* in ruins. However, property investors who saw to it that the *Lehel* ascended to one of the most sought-after property development areas in Munich – and still is – discovered the centrally located district in the 1970s.

The various water streams that shaped the quarter have long gone. Most of them were drained and filled in. The *Eisbach* is the only stream still being diverted from the Isar near the *Praterinsel* and flows underground along the House of Art where it comes back to the surface and refreshes the nude swimmers in the English Garden.

27 St. Anna im Lehel I+II

St. Anna was the minster of the monastery of the Order of the Hieronymites built in 1727. During the secularisation in 1807, the Hieronymites had to leave the monastery and it was converted into barracks. The minster with its abundant rococo decorations by the brothers Asam was named parish church. The Franciscan monks returned the barracks into a monastery in 1827, which they

still take up today. The church was destroyed entirely during the war and rebuilt in 1979. A new and distinctly larger parish church, designed by Gabriel von Seidl in neo-romanesque style, was consecrated in 1892 opposite the old minster of St. Anna. Both churches of St. Anna, including the area with its living street implementation around the churches, still form the centre of the district. St.-Anna-Platz 1 • **U** Lehel

28 Haus der Kunst (House of Art)

Adolf Hitler requested »sophisticated proportions and pure materials« when he commissioned his favourite architect Paul Ludwig Troost with the design of the *Haus der deutschen Kunst* (House of German Art). The dictator wanted an art temple in the neo-classical style and Troost delivered exactly that. The building was opened on 18th July 1937 with the inaugural exhibition »Great German Art Exhibition«. American occupation forces used the museum building as an officer's mess after the war. It was reopened in 1949 as an exhibition space with no permanent art exhibition of its own. It showcases special exhibitions from mainly contemporary world-famous artists. Prinzregentenstraße 1 • **U** Lehel or Odeonsplatz • mon–sun: 10.00–20.00/thu: 10.00–22.00

29 Eisbachsurfer (Eisbach surfers)

You do not have to travel all the way to Hawaii! The perfect wave is just around the corner and it breaks in the *Eisbach* river directly at the entrance to the English Garden. A stone step creates the standing wave of about 50cm at the emersion point of the fast flowing backwater of the river Isar, which actually runs underground up to that point. For 35 years, surfers from all over the world rode the waves here illegally but were tolerated by the police. Since 2010 surfing is officially allowed. A documentary about the *Eisbach* surfers called »Keep Surfing« opened in the cinemas in the same year. A second but tamer wave at the raft port in *Thalkirchen* is less well known to tourists but familiar to every river surfer in the world. Prinzregentenstraße 1 • **U** Lehel or Odeonsplatz

30 Englischer Garten

Elector Karl Theodor donated this lavish park to his people in 1789. The centrepiece of the English Garden was a military garden, which the Elector had built in honour to his army. It was meant as a place for meaningful outdoor recreation and agriculture during peace times. Court gardener Friedrich Ludwig Sckell planned the design of the landscape park to enormous scale on the grounds of the military garden, the royal *Hirschanger* and the adjoining landscape of the district between the Lehel and the distant village of Schwabing. The *Lehel* has since then been the gate to the English Garden which is one of the biggest urban public parks in the world. Also world-famous are the so-called *Nackerten* (nudists) as some parts of the park are officially open to nudists. After sunbathing one can enjoy a beer or shandy in Munich's second largest outdoor beer garden (7,000 seats) by the Chinese Tower (erected in 1790), people fom Munich call it »*Chinaturm*«.

31 Bayerisches Nationalmuseum (Bavarian National Museum)

The National Museum harbours a true treasure chamber filled with Bavarian and European crafts from the early Middle Ages up to today. The enormous construction by Gabriel von Seidl opened in 1900. The core of the considerable collection forms the art chambers of the Wittelsbach family. Particularly popular with visitors is the worlds most valuable and largest nativity set in the basement of the museum. Prinzregenten-straße 3 • **U** Lehel • tue–sun: 10.00–18.00/thu: 10.00–20.00

32 Lukaskirche (St. Luke's Church)

In its place was once a pier where thousands of rafts landed. The protestant *Lukaskirche* was built in 1896 after plans by Albert Schmidt in a mix of neo-gothic and neo-romanesque styles. Mariannenplatz • **S** Isartor

Basics

Its official name actually is *Isarvorstadt* but everyone just calls the district *Glockenbachviertel*. The area has a long and eventful history which was associated to the streams which used to flow through the city. A pre-industrial area with numerous mills emerged along those streams, which provided energy for these businesses. The *Isarvorstadt* remained sparsely populated for centuries due to the disastrous and reoccurring floods of the river that made life even harder in that area. During the Middle Ages, plague victims were banished to this area and the *Pechsieder* (person who boils pitch) worked here.

In the early 18th century the army discovered the *Isarvorstadt*. A military hospital and various barracks were built along the *Müllerstraße*. Barracks stood once in the spot of the current *Deutsche Museum* (German Museum) and the patent offices. It became fashionable among the city people during the 18th century to show an interest in nature and the floodplain-landscape in the *Isarvorstadt* offered plenty of that. Small country palaces among opulent gardens sprang up like mushrooms. Speaking of green: Munich's central graveyard, *Alter Südfriedhof*, was also situated there. Theatres such as the infamous *Kils Kolosseum* – Germany's largest vaudeville theatre

the *Corneliusstraße 12* and the SA (*Sturmabteilung* = Storm Detachment) practised their marches at the *Gärtnerplatz*.

By the way, the area around the *Gärtnerplatz* was entirely created on the drawing board – a circular space with roads leading away from the centre in a star shape. The tract of land belonged to the barons Eichthal. All the surrounding areas had already been developed. Eichthal built the entire district as a new development area from the ground in the 1860s.

The *Isarvorstadt* was also a vast dockland area until the construction of the new central port in 1896 but there are no traces left of that. Large numbers of rafts with timber and goods from Italy landed at the ports at the *Geyerstraße* or between the *Museumsinsel* and the *Lehel* district. Temporarily, Munich was Europe's largest raft port. The many streams, which shaped the area for a long time, were drained in 1965 as they apparently stood in the way of the construction of the underground. Only the stream *Westermühlbach* still runs partly through the district before it disappears in the canal underneath the buildings. From there on the stream is called *Glockenbach*.

After the war the area transformed itself with its strip bars and decrepit backyards to the stomping

Munich's centre: Isarvorstadt (Glockenbachviertel)

First mentioned 14th December 1812
Meaning named after the location between of the Old Town and the Isar (= suburb close to the Isar), previously »äußeres Anger-Viertel«

– already attracted visitors in the late 18th century who were looking for amusement. The numerous brothels in the area provided even more entertainment. More than 40% of all police-registered prostitutes in Munich worked between the *Gärtner-* and *Baldeplatz* in the early 20th century, which did not contribute to the reputation of the area. Neither did the settlement of slaughterhouses and butcheries in 1876. Depending on the weather, the smell of blood still makes it hard to breathe today in some streets of the area.

Many Jews from Galicia moved to the *Isarvorstadt* at the end of the 19th century due to its abundance of work in the textile and leather industries. The district became known as Munich's Jewish quarter and still remains so today. Immediately after the Second World War the synagogue in the *Reichenbachstraße* was consecrated again. Unfortunately, it was also here where the NSDAP (National Socialist German Worker's Party) began its rise as Adolf Hitler set up his party office in a backroom of a restaurant in

ground of artists and gay people of the alternative scene. Rainer Werner Fassbinder lived and worked here. Freddie Mercury logged in the *Hans-Sachs-Straße* and hosted unforgettable parties. Alternative galleries popped up everywhere at the end of the 1980s. The creative people made the *Isarvorstadt* hip and trendy and attracted business. Especially the colourful nightlife and the numerous bars turned the *Glockenbachviertel* into Munich's most desired residential and party area. The *Isarvorstadt* featured a mixed population group at the end of the 1990s with a very high share of socially disadvantaged people due to its history as an area of trade, lower class and working people, sex-orientated businesses as well as being the district of Jewish and gay people. This has changed rapidly during the past years and property and rental prices have not only rocketed but have also reached unrealistic figures.

Glücklich

Du fehlst!

33 Deutsches Museum (German Museum)

The island once served as raft port and compound for barracks. After the ports were shut down and the barracks were relocated to the north of Munich, a new purpose had to be established for the island. This was the right time for Oskar von Miller's idea of a national technical museum. Emperor Wilhelm II laid the cornerstone for the German Museum of Masterpieces of Science and Technology in 1906. Symbolically, the museum was opened on Oskar von Millers 70th birthday on 7th May 1925. The exhibition idea was revolutionary. It has been copied worldwide and still remains the same today. The museum offers an encyclopaedic overview of all areas of technology and science, apart from biology and medicine. All topics are shown and explained in plain language and understandable to everyone. Original machinery or models true to scale show technical processes and can also be operated by visitors in some cases. The collection would have filled up the rooms on the island long ago therefore branches of the museum were set up. The *Deutsches Museum* is not only the most visited museum in Munich with over 1.2 million visitors every year but also remains the worldwide leading museum for technology. Museumsinsel • **S** Isartor • daily 9.00–17.00

34 Gärtnerplatztheater (State Theatre at Gärtnerplatz)

Can a theatre function as a public company? Why not! A couple of business people set up a public company in 1863 in order to create a cultural centre in the middle of the newly developed district *Eichthal-Anger*. Architect Franz Reifenstuel designed the construction, which opened in 1865 as *Aktien-Volkstheater*. But the theatre was not a success. For a short while King Ludwig I stepped in to rescue the house but sit still did not flourish. However, it showed rapid improvement after changing the concept and turning the theatre into a stage exclusively concerned with operetta. Despite massive damages during the war, the theatre reopened in 1948 as one of the first post-war theatres in Germany. Today, the *Gärtnerplatztheater* offers musicals, operettas, operas and dance theatre and is one of the leading music stages in Germany. Much to the anger of the local residents, the circular space in front of the theatre has turned into an open-air party spot that attracts countless partygoers during the balmy summer nights. Gärtnerplatz • **U** Fraunhoferstraße

35 Alter Südfriedhof (Old South Cemetery)

The magistrate set up the first graveyard outside the city walls in 1563 in a field outside the *Sendlinger Tor* to bury the mountain of dead bodies that were victims of the Black Death when the plague ravaged through Munich without mercy. It remained Munich's only cemetery for centuries after the inner-city cemeteries had been dissolved, until 1868 when the old north cemetery was founded in the *Maxvorstadt*. No funerals haven taken place there for a long time now. Today it is Munich's oldest green space and a wonderfully beautiful oasis of tranquillity for the residents of the *Glockenbach* district. Thalkirchner Straße 17 • **U** Sendlinger Tor

36 St. Maximilian

The reason why the neo-romanesque church St. Maximilian is called »Notre Dame at the Isar« by the residents of the *Isarvorstadt*, despite the fact that the original Notre Dame in Paris is a gothic church, is due to its striking towers and not the stylistic resemblance. The church was consecrated in 1901 and is the third largest in Munich. It was heavily damaged during the war and its interior is therefore almost in-ornate today. One of the distinctive features of St. Maximilian is the high altar, which was modelled as homage to Celtic prehistoric graves of the Christendom and reminds of the Irish missionaries who introduced the Germanic and Celtic tribes to Christendom. St. Maximilian is enthroned in the centre underneath a heavy stone cross and is the missionary of the Bavarians. Balthasar Schmitt and Georg Wrba created the statues. Deutingerstraße 4 • **U** Fraunhoferstraße

37 Street Art

It is not a secret that Munich does very little to nothing for any kind of young sub-culture. For example, there are not many spaces in the city for graffiti sprayers to legally showcase their street art. Ironically, this is the city in which the German graffiti movement started in the early 1980s. Even more: in 1985 the first European »wholetrain« was sprayed in Munich (the S-Bahn in Geltendorf).

The largest and most famous areas are the walls at the slaughterhouse in the *Tumblingerstraße*, south of the *Ruppertstraße*. There is always something going on. Old graffiti disappear on a daily basis to make space for new ones. These can look extremely skilful when done by the stars of the scene or meagre when the so-called Toys (beginners) leave their work behind.

U Poccistraße

Basics

The *Ludwigsvorstadt* has a very short history. Although the area outside the *Sendlinger Tor* had been a part of Munich for a long time, it showed no noteworthy settlements. The people of Munich only came here to attend popular spectacles such as public executions. Until 1808 delinquents were hanged and witches burned at the *Galgenberg* nearby the *Hackerbrücke*. Later it became the seat of the Pschorr brewery and is today occupied by the European Patent Office. Criminals were beheaded by sword by the executioner until 1778 at the *Hauptstatt* – today the northern part of the *Hauptbahnhof* (Central Railway Station). Flogging, branding or cutting off one's extremities were the punishments for less severe crimes and were carried out in front of the crowd right by the *Sendlinger Tor*.

Thereafter, the Order of Brothers of Our Lady of Mercy opened a hospital in 1751 and laid the cornerstone for the area to become the hospital district. Four years later the Sisters of St. Elizabeth also opened a hospital. King Max I Joseph chose the area to implement the first large-scale construction project of his reign: the General Hospital, which opened in 1813. In the middle of the 19th century the district grew due to more and more hospitals where every

of the strip bars still exist today but the area between *Bayer-*, *Schiller-*, *Landwehr-* and *Goethestraße* has evolved into a small Turkish community with oriental shops, kebab stalls and import and export shops. Needless to say, the underbelly of the area around the railway station is home to drug addicts, homeless and stranded people as well as male and female prostitutes. Those who think Munich is too demure have probably never been here.

The most important day in the establishment of the *Ludwigsvorstadt* was the 17th October 1810. A horse race was organised on a field outside the city in honour of the wedding of Crown Prince Ludwig and Therese von Sachsen-Hildburghausen. This was the hour of birth for the *Oktoberfest*.

Almost 100 years later the mighty *Paulskirche* was consecrated and the wealthy people of Munich started to discover the *Ludwigsvorstadt*. They erected magnificent villas between the *Theresienwiese* and the hospital district of which many are still preserved today. The *Sonnenstraße* that divides the *Ludwigsvorstadt* from the Old Town has gone through a transformation during the past years that can be witnessed particularly at night. It is Munich's new amusement area with clubs side by side. People call

Munich's centre: Ludwigsvorstadt

First mentioned 14th December 1804 **Meaning** named after Crown Prince Ludwig, later King Ludwig I, »Vorstadt« = suburb; previously the »äußere Hackenviertel«

it the »*Feierbanane*« (party banana). It completes the gap between the party centres of the *Glockenbachviertel* with the clubs at the *Maximiliansplatz*.

specialist medical department was situated in its own building. In the early 20th century it had turned into a town of hospitals in the middle of the suburb. The entire complex is today part of the university hospital facilities.

Just like the hospital district, the central railway station with its surrounding area is like a small cosmos of its own. A new building had to be constructed after the first railway station in Munich, just a wooden shack at the time in the Maxvorstadt, had burned down in 1847. Friedrich Bürklein built the new central railway station outside the Karlstor entirely in the Italian renaissance style. The old railway building was heavily destroyed during the Second World War and was replaced by a plain new development in the 1950s. Like in any major city, the surroundings of the railway station are mainly made up of strip bars and nightclubs, gambling joints and amusement halls of all kinds. Munich's wild nightlife was legendary until the introduction of restricted areas because of the Olympic Games in 1972. Some

38 St. Paul

A terrible catastrophe happened on 17ᵗʰ December 1960 when an American plane did not climb high enough after its departure from the airport in Riem and grazed the tower of the *Paulskirche*. The plane crashed into a packed tram in the *Martin-Greif-Straße* and 52 people died. The church had been developed as part of one of the new parish churches in the continuously growing suburbs. The magnificent neo-gothic building was consecrated in 1906. **U** Theresienwiese

39 Theresienwiese

Five days after Crown Prince Ludwig, who later became King Ludwig I, had married the Princess Therese of Sachsen-Hildburghausen, a big horse race was hosted on 17th October 1810 at the meadow *Sendlinger Wiese*. The horse race was the birth of the *Oktoberfest* and the meadow was officially renamed after the bride to »*Theresiens Wiese*«. Not only is the *Theresienwiese* the venue for the *Oktoberfest* but it also hosts the *Frühlingsfest*, the *Winter-Tollwood-Festival* and a large flea market every April. **U** Theresienwiese

40 Oktoberfest

It was 17th October 1810. In honour of the wedding of Crown Prince Ludwig and Therese von Sachsen-Hildburghausen the banker Andreas Michael Dall'Armi organised a horse race at the large meadow *Sendlinger Wiese* just outside of the city. Almost the entire city of Munich attended the spectacle, which was hosted again in the following year by request of the Crown Prince. The tradition of the *Oktoberfest* was born. At first the horse race gave the *Oktoberfest* a more sportive character however, soon the first merry-go-rounds appeared and various »Traiteurs« (the forerunner of today's party caterers) supplied the people with refreshments. The city council decided in 1819 that the *Oktoberfest* was to take place every year. The meadow on which it was hosted was named *Theresienwiese* or short »Wiesn« in honour of the Crown Princess. Towards the end of the 19th century the *Oktoberfest* had transformed itself more and more into a »fair for the public«. Today the *Oktoberfest* attracts around 6 million visitors from all over the world every year. Mostly Italians, Australians and US-Americans. By the way, the trend to wear the national costumes is not a tradition but a recent fashion. City people do not wear traditional costumes. Until the end of the 1990s most Munich folk went to the »Wiesn« dressed in normal clothes and many ranted about the traditional costume looking like fancy dress. **U** Theresienwiese

Basics

After the city walls had been demolished, Bavaria's King Maximilian I Joseph elected the area between the *Karlstor* and the *Schwabinger Tor* to be an ideal space for new housing estates. Sufficient construction space was also available around the most important street, the *Fürstenweg*, situated towards the West. Villas with large gardens were to be built at the *Fürstenweg* (today *Brienner Straße*). In contrast, the north of the *Fürstenweg* was developed less spaciously. The district was to be made up of a street grid and poky roads.

But what was to happen outside the *Schwabinger Tor*? Suddenly Crown Prince Ludwig started to get involved. As by magic he introduced architect Leo von Klenze. Klenze, who was like the Crown Prince a fan of antique architecture, was to implement Ludwig's concepts for the *Maxvorstadt*: the so-called *Isar-Athen*. Klenze removed the *Schwabinger Tor* and levelled the city walls to create the square *Odeonsplatz*. He also planned the new glamorous boulevard *Ludwigstraße*. However, Klenze only succeeded partially as Ludwig I, who was by now King, was fickle and had found a new favourite already: Friedrich von Gärtner. Gärtner finished the concept after his own taste and also built the national library, the universi-

living but also for studying. Ludwig I relocated the university from Landshut to Munich in 1826 and Munich became a student town. The army also occupied large areas in the *Maxvorstadt*. People in uniform were very common on the streets. The barracks also boosted the business of brothels in the *Maxvorstadt*. Loose women and dangerous men as well as students and artists – no surprise that the *Maxvorstadt* had turned to a bohemian quarter towards the end of the 19th century. The protagonists commuted between the *Maxvorstadt* and *Schwabing* and quickly everything north of the *Odeonsplatz* belonged to *Schwabing*. This stuck and many people today still refer to the *Maxvorstadt* as *Schwabing*.

Wild parties took place in the bar *Simplicissimus* in the *Türkenstraße* and in the *Café Stefanie* in the *Theresienstraße* on the corner to *Amalienstraße*. Kandinsky invented abstraction, Franz Marc shocked with blue horses, Thomas Mann wrote his novels – »Schwabylon« attracted artists from all over the world. The bohemian life came to an end with the First World War and Hitler's rise began.

The *Maxvorstadt* was left in a field of rubble after allied bombers ended the twelve years of Hitler's dictatorship. The city planned office buildings instead of

Munich's centre: Maxvorstadt

First mentioned 14th December 1812 as »Maximiliansvorstadt« (Maximilian's suburb)
Meaning named after Bavaria's first King Maximilian I Joseph, previously »äußeres Kreuzviertel« as part of the Kreuzviertel

ty as well as the *Feldherrnhalle* (Field Marshal's Hall) and the *Siegestor* (Victory Gate).

There it was, Ludwig's monumental avenue with two enclosed and solid rows of houses with no gardens and lots of plaster. And what was around it? Not much apart from fields and meadows, some garden villas and barracks. The people of Munich could not believe it. The king had built a road in the middle of nowhere, leading nowhere.

Klenze did not only leave his traces in the *Ludwigstraße*. He also designed the *Königsplatz* with the *Glyptothek* (museum) and the *Propyläen* (city gate). He built the Old Pinakothek and created the 29m high obelisk at the square *Karolinenplatz*. Some of the small palaces along the *Brienner Straße* still give a little impression of how the *Maxvorstadt* might have looked in the past. The flair of the former garden estate was lost already in the 19th century. Construction from that point on was high, quick and cheap.

The *Maxvorstadt*, however, was not only an area for

residential buildings for the reconstruction. Simultaneously, the university expanded into the district and outsourced departments appeared everywhere. Munich was to become a traffic friendly city, which was the catch phrase at the time in order present oneself as an up-to-date city planner. Therefore, the ring road *Altstadtring* was built cutting straight through the *Maxvorstadt*. Only from the middle of the 1970s people started to rethink. Especially because of the university in the *Maxvorstadt*, the district regained its status as popular residential area in the 1980s most of all among the students. The ratio of 20–30 year olds is still extremely high. The »Schwabing effect« worked again. Slowly the creative scene returned and the bars became more colourful and interesting. Due to its central location, good transport links and high recreational value because of the English Garden, the property market has targeted the *Maxvorstadt* heavily during the past years and property prices have rocketed into the sky.

41 Justizpalast (Palace of Justice)

He tried to apply for the job to build the *Reichstag* in Berlin but he only made it to second place in the competition. Hence, architect Friedrich Thiersch was even more delighted when he was commissioned to design the Palace of Justice in Munich. To outshine the *Reichstag* in Berlin, Thiersch decided to build even bigger and more impressive by adding an even larger glass dome. However, it became obvious after the opening in 1897 that there still was a lack of space despite of the large scale of the building. Therefore, Thiersch was again commissioned in 1902 to extend the building. He decided on an entirely different style of building and created directly next to the old neo-baroque building a new building in the austere brick gothic style, which was completed in 1905. **U/S** Karlsplatz

42 Wittelsbacherbrunnen (Wittelsbach Fountain)

A truly splendid fellow – the brawny athlete Johann Göhringer from Munich had travelled all over the world with the circus Barnum & Bailey. And he can still be adored today because he was the model for the »destroyer« by the sculptor Adolf von Hildebrand. This is the statue on the left of the Wittelsbach Fountain at the *Lenbachplatz*. He rides on an allegorical creature; half horse half fish and throws a heavy stone up into the air. The fountain, which was erected between 1893 and 1895, is an allegory about the elementary power of water, which can be destructive or beneficial. The female figure on the right-hand side is the »symbol for the beneficial power of water that fertilises the land«. The fountain was a donation by the city of Munich in remembrance to the completion of a new high-pressure, fresh water pipe from the valley *Mangfalltal* in the year 1883. **U/S** Karlsplatz

43 St. Bonifaz

Originally, there was supposed to be a house of prayer opposite the museum *Glyptothek* but King Ludwig I changed his mind and ordered architect Georg Friedrich Ziebland to build a church near the *Königsplatz* in the style of the Basilica of St. Apollinare in Ravenna. It took 15 years to complete the basilica with its five naves. The church was christened in 1850 in the name of St. Bonifaz, the apostle of Germany. The pastoral care was given to the monks of the Order of St. Benedict and a monastery was built for them behind the church. For the monks to be able to earn a living in the city, Ludwig I endowed them with the monastery *Andechs* including the surrounding land. It was formed in 1455 and is located by the lake *Ammersee*. St. Bonifaz is now much smaller due to heavy destruction during the war and King Ludwig I and his Queen Therese are buried in the church. Karlstraße 34 • **U** Königsplatz

44 Lenbachhaus

»I am thinking of building myself a palace which will outshine all others. The powerful centres of European art shall be connected here to the present«, wrote Franz von Lenbach in 1885. Lenbach (1836–1904) could afford such immodesty because he was viewed as the King of Painters at the end of the 19th century. However, his artistic skills have since been regarded as less considerable. He possessed two very essential skills which were important in the art market: self-promotion in combination with self-staging and how to play the game of intrigue. Princes and rulers equally consulted Lenbach regularly.

Architect Gabriel von Seidl designed the prestigious art domicile into which Lenbach moved in 1896. Lenbach's widow bequeathed the villa including all paintings of the artist to the city of Munich in 1924. Today, the civic gallery inside the Lenbachhaus is a crowd-puller primarily because of its extensive collection of the Blue Rider group with masterpieces from Kandinsky to Marc. The painter Gabriele Münter, who was the former lover of Kandinsky, laid the cornerstone for the group. She left her precious Kandinsky-collection to the city of Munich in 1957. Since the 1970s the museum also showcases important contemporary artists. In 2013, the Lenbachhaus reopened after lengthy reconstruction with a spectacular extension by Foster & Partners. Luisenstraße 33 •
U Königsplatz • tue–sun: 10.00–18.00

45 Königsplatz

Originally, the city of Munich finished at the *Königsplatz*. The architect Karl von Fischer designed the square based on antique models in Athens. Vivid green was to set a worthy frame for the constructions ruled by classic precision. However, Ludwig I, still Crown Prince at the time, did not trust Fischer to execute his ideal of the *Isar-Athen*. He held a competition and commissioned Leo von Klenze in 1815 with the construction of his Hellenic temple in the Ionic style. The *Glyptothek* opened in 1830 and was Munich's first public museum. Here, Ludwig I showed his continuously growing collection of antique statues to the public. At first a church was to be erected opposite the *Glyptothek* and then a national library. Eventually Ludwig I decided that a building devoted to the promotion of art and trade in Bavaria would be the best addition to the *Glyptothek*. He commissioned Georg Friedrich von Ziebland with the construction of the present *Antikensammlung* (Antiquities Collection) in the style of a Corinthian temple. The work on the building took place from 1838 until 1848. Now there was the Ionic *Glyptothek* and the Corinthian exhibition hall but missing was the third of the architectural orders: the Doric order. As a symbolic city gate to the west, Leo von Klenze started the construction of the *Propyläen* after the model of the Acropolis in Athens. Ludwig I had long abdicated during its official inauguration in 1862 and had paid for the construction out of his own pocket. **U** Königsplatz

46 Technische Universität München – TUM

Humanistic education is a good thing but a bit more practical experience might not go amiss for the students of the new era of the industrialisation. So, the Polytechnic Institute opened in Munich in 1827. King Ludwig II raised the status of the Polytechnic Institute in 1868 to be equal with that of a university. Architect Gottfried von Neureuther designed the building in the *Arcisstraße*. In 1875, Carl von Linde opened Germany's first mechanical laboratory where Rudolf Diesel also later studied. Along with Diesel, the most famous graduate of the university was Oskar von Miller, who was the initiator of the *Deutsches Museum*. The university's landmark, the tower created by Friedrich von Thiersch at the *Gabelsbergerstraße*, was built in 1916 and can be seen even from afar. Bombs destroyed almost 80% of the buildings in the *Maxvorstadt* during the Second World War. In 1957 the TUM opened Germany's first research reactor in *Garching*. From then on the third campus in the small town north of Munich was extended along with the campuses in the *Maxvorstadt* and *Weihenstephan*. Today the TUM offers 142 study courses to almost 31,000 students and belongs to Germany's elite universities along with the *LMU* (Ludwig-Maximilians-University). Arcisstraße 21
• U Theresienstraße

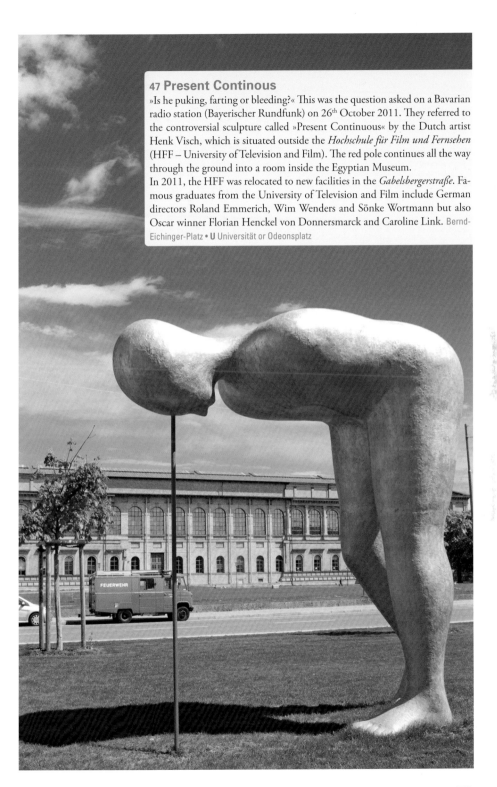

47 Present Continous

»Is he puking, farting or bleeding?« This was the question asked on a Bavarian radio station (Bayerischer Rundfunk) on 26th October 2011. They referred to the controversial sculpture called »Present Continuous« by the Dutch artist Henk Visch, which is situated outside the *Hochschule für Film und Fernsehen* (HFF – University of Television and Film). The red pole continues all the way through the ground into a room inside the Egyptian Museum.

In 2011, the HFF was relocated to new facilities in the *Gabelsbergerstraße*. Famous graduates from the University of Television and Film include German directors Roland Emmerich, Wim Wenders and Sönke Wortmann but also Oscar winner Florian Henckel von Donnersmarck and Caroline Link. Bernd-Eichinger-Platz • **U** Universität or Odeonsplatz

48 Pinakotheken

The largest plot to exhibit art in the world awaits you: nowhere else are so many museums per square meter as in the *Maxvorstadt*. The *Pinakotheken* (art galleries) with their considerable collections make up a significant part of that.

Wilhelm IV provided the basis of the collection of the *Alte Pinakothek* (Old Pinacotheca). He had started to invite famous painters to his court in Munich from 1528. The Electors Maximilian I and Maximilian II Emanuel enthusiastically collected art and brought great masterpieces by Rubens or van Dyk to Munich. The eagerness to collect art among the Bavarian rulers continued. Particularly, King Ludwig I collected everything in terms of art on which he could lay his hands. Ludwig I also saw it in his duty to educate the national public and wanted to make the royal collection accessible to everyone. He commissioned Leo von Klenze with the construction of a museum. On Raffaels birthday, the 7th of April 1826, the foundation was laid for a museum of such proportion the world had never seen before. Klenze created an architectural sensation, which is still copied today in museums throughout the world: he installed skylights. The *Alte Pinakothek* was closed during the Second World War and the precious collection was put into storage for safekeeping outside of Munich. This proved to be a lucky move to conserve the priceless works when bombs destroyed the building severely. The reconstruction began in 1952 and as a reminder of the war the wall along the south façade was deliberately rebuilt only partially. The gallery was reopened in 1957.

Ludwig I also showed an interest in modern and contemporary art. He commissioned Friedrich von Gärtner and August von Voit with the construction of a *Neue Pinakothek* (New Pinacotheca) and in 1853 the first museum in the world for modern art opened. However, the bombs hit the *Neue Pinako-*

thek hard and its ruins had to be removed entirely in 1949. Architect Alexander von Branca designed the new *Neue Pinakothek*, which opened in 1981. Today the *Neue Pinakothek* contains over 3,000 paintings and 300 sculptures of the 19th and early 20th century.

The collection of modern art started rather modestly and can be found today in the *Pinakothek der Moderne*. The collection only consisted of six paintings after the Second World War because of the Nazis' intolerance and atrocity towards art. Further acquisitions and donations helped the collection to grow. The archives started to burst and what was missing was the exhibition space to showcase the collection. Eventually, it was decided to build the *Pinakothek der Moderne* on the former grounds of the Turkish barracks. Only the gate to the barracks in the *Türkenstraße* remains today. The architect Stephan Braunfels designed the ample building, which opened on 16th September 2002. The *Pinakothek der Moderne* accommodates the collection of *Modern Art* but also the *Collection of Drawings and Engravings*, the *New Collection* and the *Museum of Architecture*.

The latest addition to the museum is the *Museum Brandhorst*. The top-class collection by Udo Brandhorst, the heir to the Henkel enterprise and his wife Anette, consists of over 700 great works by world famous artists of the 20th century. Among them Pablo Picasso, Cy Twombly, Andy Warhol and Siegmar Polke. The museum by architects Sauerbruch Hutton opened in spring 2009 next to the *Pinakothek der Moderne*. **Alte Pinakothek** Barer Straße 27 • tue–sun: 10.00–18.00/tue: 10.00–20.00 • **Neue Pinakothek** Barer Straße 29 • wed–mon: 10.00–18.00/wed: 10.00–20.00 • **Pinakothek der Moderne** Barer Straße 40 • tue–sun: 10.00–18.00/thu: 10.00–20.00 • **Museum Brandhorst** Theresienstraße 35 a • tue–sun: 10.00–18.00/thu: 10.00–20.00 • **U** Theresienstraße or Universität or Odeonsplatz

49 Alter Nördlicher Friedhof (Old North Cemetery)

Building a cemetery right in the centre of the brand new *Maxvorstadt*? Unthinkable! People feared a dark and chilling place. But all the protests were in vain. Munich's only cemetery, the Old South Cemetery outside the *Sendlinger Tor* was bursting at its seams. Work for the new cemetery started in 1866. About 62,000 people would find their last resting place there in the centuries to come. Funerals were then prohibited in 1939 because Adolf Hitler had planned to set up his retirement home on the grounds of the cemetery. Today the Old North Cemetery is popular with the local residents of the Maxvorstadt for recreational purposes, a green and calm spot in between dense city roads. Arcisstraße 45 • U Josephsplatz

50 Ludwig-Maximilians-Universität (LMU)

The university's history began in 1472. Ludwig der Reiche (Louis the Rich) opened a university in Ingolstadt. In the 18th century, the university was regarded as one of the most modern and advanced of its kind in the whole of Europe. In 1800, invading French troops prompted Elector Max IV Joseph to have the university relocated to Landshut. The university in Landshut counted to one of the largest in Germany in 1826 with almost 1,000 students. In the same year, King Ludwig I ordered the relocation of the university to Munich. The new main building located at the *Geschwister-Scholl-Platz* was ready in 1840 and was built by architect Friedrich von Gärtner. The year 1900 saw the first women to graduate from a university when the Scottish students Maria Ogilvie-Gordon and Agnes Kelly received their doctorate. The university expanded so rapidly after the Second World War that more departments had to be outsourced from the *Maxvorstadt*. Almost 50,000 students enrolled for the winter term in 2011/2012 at the Ludwig-Maximilians-University making it the second largest university in Germany after the Open University in Hagen. The LMU is, just like the TUM (Polytechnic Institute), one of the elite universities and is regarded as the best university in Germany. Geschwister-Scholl-Platz 1 • **U** Universität

The Nazi-Quarter

When the amateur painter Adolf Hitler moved into rental accommodation in the *Schleißheimer Straße 34* at the end of May 1913, he felt as he had arrived in the mecca of German art. He shared a room with a friend with whom he had already shared a hostel for homeless people in Vienna. Hitler painted Munich's landmarks and sold them on to tourists. He was discharged from the Austrian army as unfit but joined the Bavarian army during the First World War. After the war he worked as an informer for the intelligence service where his talent for speeches was detected and he joined the *Deutsche Arbeiterpartei DAP* (German worker's party) in 1919, the preceding party of the *NSDAP* (National Socialist German Workers Party). He shaped the party significantly and became its most important agitator and mastermind. It looked like the »brown regime« (brown was the colour of the party uniforms) had ended after Hitler's failed putsch on 9th November 1923 outside the *Feldherrnhalle*. But this was only the beginning and events started to take place mainly in the *Maxvorstadt*; to be exact in the parlour of his committed supporter, the publisher Bruckmann, at the *Karolinenplatz 5*. Hitler opened the branch office of the NSDAP in the *Schellingstraße 50*. He bought the *Palace Barlow* at the *Brienner Straße* in 1931 with generous donations from international benefactors (among them Prescott Bush, father and respectively grandfather to the two US-presidents to come). It became the national headquarter of the NSDAP,

the so-called *Braunes Haus* (Brown House). Hitler was mostly fascinated by the antique architecture of the *Königsplatz*. It was the venue for the book burning by the Nazis and Hitler had the square transformed into a marching field by plastering it with 21,545 granite paving stones. The people of Munich called the square »Plattensee« (lake of flat slabs) because the water did not drain off after heavy rain. Only since 1988, has the square been returned to its original green state. The *Führerbau* (today University for Music), the *Verwaltungsbau* (administration) of the NSDAP (today Central Institute for Art History) as well as the two *Ehrentempel* (memorials) for the 16 rebels killed during the Hitler putsch, were set up at the edge of the *Königsplatz*. The Nazis held ghastly commemorations here. In time, Hitler's henchmen occupied everything between the *Karl-*, *Barer-*, Ga*belsberger-* and *Arcisstraße*. Every important NS organisation moved to the *Maxvorstadt*, such as *Kraft durch Freude* (Strength through Joy), the leaders of the *SA* (Assault Division) and the Central Office for the Execution of the Four Year Plan. They also created an underground city, which connected important buildings through a tunnel system with various different rooms. The majority of residential homes of the *Maxvorstadt* were reduced to rubble by the bombs of the Second World War and of all things these pretentious Hitler constructions ironically survived unharmed. The *Braune Haus* (Brown House) however was destroyed. The American allies blew up the *Ehrentempel* in 1947. A NS-Documentation Centre will open in 2014 where the Brown House used to stand.

München. Braunes Haus mit Führerhaus und Ehrentempel.

Resistance against the regime of terror

Hans Scholl and Alexander Schmorell wrote in their first flyer by the resistance group called »*Weiße Rose*« (White Rose): »Does not every German citizen feel ashamed of their government today?« and called for passive resistance against the NS dictatorship. Through heroes like them the »District of the Movement« also became the »District of Ccounter Movement«. But the siblings Hans and Sophie Scholl were betrayed when they were seen handing out their seventh flyer at the Ludwig-Maximilians University on 18th February 1943. The members of the non-violent resistance group »White Rose«, set up by the siblings Scholl and professor Kurt Huber, were executed. Stone copies of their flyers are embedded into the ground as memorial at the main entrance of the university. Also in the *Maxvorstadt*, in the *Türkenstraße*, lived *Georg Elser* who attempted to kill Hitler with a bomb on 8th November 1939 at the pub *Bürgerbräukeller*. Members of the group »*Freiheitsaktion Bayern*« failed in an armed riot against the NS-Leaders during the last days of war and were murdered at the Ministry of Agriculture at the *Ludwigstraße*. Various memorials honour these brave and courageous people today: Geschwister-Scholl-Platz 1, Türkenstraße 68, Ludwigstraße 2 • **U** Universität and Odeonsplatz

51 St. Ludwig

»I tell you this work is truly disgraceful«, ranted King Ludwig I. The monarch had just visited the completed *Ludwigskirche* for the first time and was outraged about the world's second largest altar wall painting, which had been created by painter Peter Cornelius in 1839/40. His depiction of the Last Judgement was far too dark and dreary according to the furious King Ludwig I. The fresco disaster ended the collaboration between the regent and Cornelius who thereupon moved to Berlin. Ludwig I had the monumental church built by Friedrich von Gärtner and had paid 100,000 guilder from his own pocket for the venture because the city had dismissed the construction plans as too expensive. In 1844, Archbishop Lothar Anselm von Gebsattel consecrated the *Ludwigskirche*, which Gärtner had designed in form of a three-aisled Byzantine basilica with the basic geometric figure of the cross of tau.

Ludwigstraße 20 • **U** Universität

52 Staatsbibliothek (National Library)

A sovereign with an appreciation in art laid the foundation: Duke Albrecht V bought the private library of the Austrian chancellor Johann Albrecht Widmanstetter in 1558. Few years later, Albrecht V purchased a library with 10,000 books from the Augsburg based Patrician Johann Jakob Fugger. The Munich library quickly became one of the most significant book collections in Europe. Albrecht's successors eagerly continued to collect books. Then in 1802, the secularisation came and important books and precious manuscripts from around 150 convents became part of the royal library. The Munich Library was the second largest library Europe's in 1818, after the Bibliothèque Nationale in Paris.

In 1832, Ludwig I commissioned his architect Friedrich von Gärtner with the construction of the »most magnificent building in Munich«: the National Library. The building at the *Ludwigstraße* includes two courtyards making it Germany's largest brick building with 153m in length, 78m in depth and 24m in height. Ludwig von Schwanthaler created the four stone statues by the outside staircase, which the people of Munich named »The Four Wise Men«. They refer to the diversity of science, depicting Thukydides – founder of scientific history, Homer – author of the »Iliad« and »Odyssey«, Aristotle – philosopher and teacher of Alexander the Great as well as Hippocrates – most famous ancient physician. Almost 10 million books make up the total portfolio, among them 93,800 manuscripts. Ludwigstraße 16 • **U** Universität • reading room: 8.00–24.00

53 Siegestor (Victory Gate)

King Ludwig I hated the French but he was lacking the funds for a war. Nevertheless, Ludwig I planned to prove his intention to conquer France in a tremendous fashion. He ordered Friedrich von Gärtner to create a triumphal arch, based on the Arch of Constantine in Rome, as finishing point of the *Ludwigstraße*. On top of the arch is a bronze statue of Bavaria with a lion-quadriga facing away from the city. Ludwig I ordered that the quadriga should never be turned around. During the construction in 1843 and 1850, Ludwig had to abdicate and the architect Gärtner passed away. The gate lived up to its name, long after Ludwig's death, when in 1871 German troops returned to Munich after victory over France. After sustaining heavy damage in the Second World War, the gate was reconstructed but restored only partially. The inscription on the southern side says »Dedicated to victory, destroyed by war, reminding of peace«. Ludwigstraße • **U** Universität

54 Academy of Fine Arts

Those who wanted to study art during the 19th century came to Munich. The Bavarian metropolis was regarded in Central Europe as most important city of art. Munich's primary export product was beer followed by art, mainly genre and historical painting. Gottfried von Neureuther designed the New Academy in 1886 to accommodate the many art students from all over the world. After historical painting went out of fashion, the academy began to bloom more than ever and even caused an artistic revolution. This was the place where the pioneers of modern age studied: Giorgio de Chirico, Wassily Kandinsky, Paul Klee, Alfred Kubin, Franz Marc, Christian Schad and Lovis Corinth – only to name a few. However, Munich's artistic era ended with the First World War. The modern extension was completed in 2005 after plans by Coop Himmelb(l)au. Akademiestraße 2 • **U** Universität

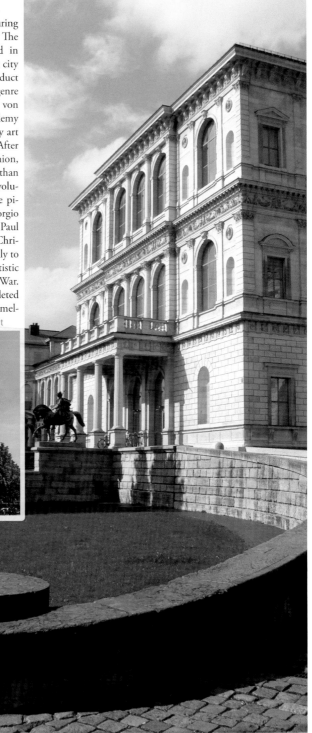

Basics

A popular area for nightlife and living – *Schwabing* used to be just that in the 1960s and 1970s but was replaced in the 1980s by the district *Haidhausen*. Everyone who was young and trendy – or at least thought they were – moved here. The old workers district enjoyed a revival as the young and trendy district of Munich. Even though the district of *Haidhausen* is much older than Munich.

For centuries the sleepy village was hidden away until Munich's foundation in 1158, because the new trading route for the precious commodity salt cut straight through *Haidhausen*. The road to Vienna became a lifeline. Coachmen and traders had to be catered for. A new source of income soon developed. The people of Munich decided in the 15th century to build their homes and the city walls from stone after many disastrous fires. Artificial stone had to be produced such as bricks made from clay because there were no appropriate naturals stones available in the region. However, clay was available in abundance in *Haidhausen*. Munich started from 1443 gradually to buy off the lands, which provided clay, from the residents of Haidhausen. When the grounds had been depleted, the land was given back to the farmers for recultivation. Large numbers of Italian migrant workers laboured in the

the 17th century. Munich attracted more and more workers from the suburbs who could not afford the expensive city and who found cheap housing in the villages around Munich. With the industrialisation in the 19th century more work-seekers arrived and the conditions in those living quarters started to become increasingly catastrophic. Entire families had to share a minimal space with small rooms but also had to share an outhouse and a pump well. Many were starving. It was the ideal feeding ground for plagues such as cholera. Beggars and scallywags were up to no good. The city of Munich incorporated *Haidhausen* in 1854. One of the reasons was that it was hoped that the police would have better chances to catch the criminals. The housing shortage found its high point in the early 20th century. The east railway station made *Haidhausen* popular as industrial site and brought even more workers into the village. In order to improve the housing situation, the city of Munich prohibited the construction of worker dwellings, acquired the existing ones and demolished them. Only modern tenements were allowed. The last large settlement of worker dwellings had to make way to an extension of the hospital *Klinikum rechts der Isar* in the 1950s. Today the clinic, with its

Munich's east: Haidhausen

First mentioned 12th February 808 as »Heidhusir« **Meaning** Häuser auf der Heide = Houses on the Heath **Incorporation** 1st October 1854

brickyards up to 16 hours a day in the late 19th and 20th century. Among them were many children.

The exposed position along the salt route just outside of Munich caused the people of *Haidhausen* an enormous disadvantage. No matter what kind of war just went on, *Haidhausen* always suffered. Many reasons could have been the case such as the access roads to Munich were easy to block from there, houses could be used as accommodation for the soldiers and barns and sheds could be looted or maybe because the view from the *Gasteig* over the city was an ideal position for the cannons. Particularly bad for the village was the Thirty-Year-War when the Swedish under King Gustav Adolf advanced towards Munich from the north via *Haidhausen*. For centuries the village *Haidhausen* consisted only of the church *St. Johannis Baptist*, four large farms, the *Palace Törring-Seefeld* – where the overlords lived – as well as the *Palace Preysing* and the small *Palace Haidenau* (none of the palaces and farms exist today). However, slums surrounded the village. The so-called *Herbergssiedlungen*, very simple worker dwellings, emerged in

individual departments and institutes, is part of the Technical University Munich (TUM).

Haidhausen also became a central hub for beer within the beer metropolis Munich. Because beer had to be stored in cool cellars, the raised banks of the Isar at the *Gasteig* proved to be of service. The hill *Rosenheimer Berg* was soon riddled with beer cellars. In 1850, more than 50 beer cellars existed there, virtually the party hot spot of the 19th century of which only the brewery and restaurant *Hofbräukeller* at the *Wiener Platz* remain today. The beer cellars were also popular with Adolf Hitler who used the venues for his political agitations. The fascist hate sheet »*Völkischer Beobachter*« also found its origin in *Haidhausen* and was originally the neighbourhood newsletter »*Münchner Beobachter*«.

Haidhausen was mainly spared during the war and showed very little destruction. The district became a popular residential area in the late 20th century due to its high number of renovated historic buildings. New housing developments emerged on the grounds of the former industrial premises. Today, its lively centre is the market at the *Wiener Platz*, founded in 1899, which is the smallest of the four outdoor food markets in Munich.

55 Friedensengel (Angel of Peace)

The *Friedensengel* stands at the border between *Haidhausen* and *Bogenhausen*. The Angel of Peace is a reminder of the 25 peaceful years after the Franco-German war in 1870/71. The foundation stone was laid in 1896. If one approaches from the bridge *Prinzregentenbrücke*, a central fountain greets with putti riding on four waterspout dolphins. From there two staircases lead to the elevated viewing point where a 38m high Corinthian column with the Angel of Peace rises into the sky. The 6m high figure is a replica of the Nike of Paeonius, in effect making it a Goddess of Victory. The small temple at the bottom of the column contains portraits of regents and generals as well as four gold mosaics depicting the allegories of war and piece, victory and blessing for the culture. Europaplatz 1 • U Prinzregentenplatz

56 Villa Stuck

As if artists only become famous after their death and their heirs become rich! Franz von Stuck (1863–1928) managed to live very well of his talent, just like Franz von Lenbach and Friedrich von Kaulbach. The miller's son rose to become a highly paid star of the artistic world. Stuck loved to provoke and his erotic paintings always contained a hint of scandal. He designed the villa including its interior and furniture, which he had built in 1898 at the *Prinzregentenstraße*. In 1915 he extended the villa with an artist studio.

Since 1992, the villa belongs to the city of Munich. In the same year, the Museum Villa Stuck opened. Apart from the historic living quarters and studio facilities as well as objects from the 1900s, the museum shows alternating special exhibitions. Prinzregentenstraße 60 • **U** Prinzregentenplatz • tue–sun: 11.00–18.00

57 Maximilianeum

King Maximilian II wanted to follow suit to his father Ludwig I and set a course of urban accents. So, he had the boulevard *Maximilianstraße* built for him in 1853, which runs from the city centre to the river Isar. He requested a monumental construction opposite of the Isar as a worthy conclusion of the boulevard. He also planned a student's foundation for gifted students. The land was bought in 1857 and the construction work after plans by architect Friedrich Bürklein began. Because of the poor quality of the construction grounds by the banks of the Isar, the *Maximilianeum* was only opened in 1874. Contemporary residents considered the construction with criticism. The Swiss art historic Jacob Burckhardt mocked it as »cardboard botch« adding »and when you see the pathetic rear side it makes you feel completely faint«. The *Maximilianeum* received a new lodger after the Second World War: the homeless Bavarian Parliament. The Parliament was opened there with a ceremonial act on 11th January 1949. A month later, the Bavarian Senate also moved in. The *Maximilianeum* mainly still serves as a student's foundation today. Max-Planck-Straße 1 • **U** Max-Weber-Platz

58 Wiener Platz

Although it is situated on the edge of *Haidhausen*, it is still regarded as the heart of the district: the *Wiener Markt* (Viennese market) also known as *Markt am Wiener Platz*. Its name derives from the fact that it was located along the historic route to Vienna. It is the smallest of the four permanent food markets in Munich along with the *Viktualienmarkt*, *Pasinger Viktualienmarkt* and the *Elisabethmarkt* in *Schwabing*. The group »*Freunde Haidhausen*« donated the maypole in 2003. Traders do not need a lease agreement but an »allocation«. New applicants advance up the waiting list as soon as a stall becomes available whereas the stall has to be assorted with the same products in order to keep the market balance.

Directly located at the *Wiener Platz* is the brewery and restaurant *Hofbräukeller*. From 1896, the royal beer was not brewed in the *Hofbräuhaus* anymore but was now made in *Haidhausen*. The brewery was relocated from *Haidhausen* to *Riem* in 1988 after a major fire, which destroyed most of the production sites. Today only the restaurant and the popular beer garden remind of the once glorious time of the beer industry in *Haidhausen*.

The *Hofbräukeller* was also host to an absolute low point in world history: the mass murderer and dictator Adolf Hitler held his first public and party-political speech there in front of 100 listeners on 16th October 1919. Wiener Platz • **U** Max-Weber-Platz

59 Herbergen (workers dwellings)

How romantic! Small houses that are still preserved throughout *Haidhausen* and the districts *Au* and *Giesing*. They are often lovingly decorated and contain small gardens, which today make us think of cute little messengers from the time we often like to refer to as the »good old times«. As if!

These houses are the remains of once large dwellings for the destitute population. To live in these dwellings meant that more than one family lived in one house, often just sharing one room. That room was generally the personal property of the inhabitants. In a manner of speaking those rooms were owner-occupied properties. Especially the poorest of the poor ran into large debts in order to own their own property. The hygienic conditions defied description. Water had to be collected from a well and the toilets were stinking outhouses used by a number of people. The rooms were tiny, dark and damp with low ceilings and almost not heatable.

The houses were usually made from timber, which started to rot quickly. No wonder that these dwellings were the perfect breeding ground for disease. Only a third of the new-borns survived and half of them did not make it to their first birthday.

Nevertheless, these dwellings were highly desired because many workers were looking for a home close to the city from where they could commute to work. The large settlements formed a semi-circle around the actual village of *Haidhausen*. Some dwellings were also set up within the village. One of them is the still preserved *Kriechbaumhof* from 1760. Large tenements replaced the smaller accommodations increasingly from the 1880s. Eventually the city of Munich prohibited the construction of those workers dwellings. The settlements were demolished on a large-scale during the coming years. Only a few of the quarters remained for the city's historic background. The historic photos on the left show some of those dwellings in *Haidhausen* and *Au*. You find those dwellings at: An der Kreppe, Wiener Platz, Preysingstraße 58 + 71 • **U** Max-Weber-Platz

München – Am Paulanerplatz.

60 Müllersches Volksbad (Mueller's Public Baths)
Not many accommodations were equipped with a bathroom.
The engineer Karl von Müller donated these public swimming
baths to allow even ordinary people to take a bath once in a while. Architect Carl Hocheder, inspired by roman thermal springs
and oriental hammams, created the art-nouveau building within
four years, which was the largest public swimming bath in the
world when it opened on 9ᵗʰ May 1901. Simultaneously, it was
the first public indoor swimming pool in Munich. Elaborate
wall paintings, a bronze statue inside the main pool, opulent decorations from iron and wood make the *Müllersche Volksbad* today one of the public baths in the world well worth seeing. The
original 86 bathtubs and 22 shower baths however, have long
gone. Rosenheimer Straße 1 • **S** Rosenheimer Platz • daily 7.30–23.00

61 Gasteig

What to do with the lepers? Get them out of the city up on to the hill *Gasteig*! The steep hill belonged to the part of the city just outside the city walls. The city set up the leper's house around 1204, including the chapel St. Nikolai, today called *Gasteigkircherl*. The sick had to wear black coats with wide white collars in order to be immediately noticeable. At first they had to beg for a living but the regents and the rich townspeople devotedly donated. The hospice soon owned enough land and estates in order to survive economically. Leprosy was widely contained in the 18th century and the hospice took in all sorts of sick people. The leper's house was demolished in 1863. Only the St. Nikolai church and the *Altötting* chapel remain today.

The hill was also suited for military purposes. During almost every war the enemy troops took their positions there. Just like on 15th May 1632 when Swedish troops threatened Munich during the Thirty-Year-War. The negotiators of the city travelled up to the *Gasteig* hill and bowed to the Swedish king Karl Gustav. They surrendered the city under the conditions that Munich may not be ransacked.

Opposite the leper's house used to be a poor house and later a home for the elderly. Behind it were the enormous premises of the brewery *Bürgerbräu*. Adolf Hitler liked to use the beer cellars in *Haidhausen* for his appearances. The so-called Beer Putsch was staged on 8th November 1923 at the *Bürgerbräu* but was violently prevented. The carpenter Georg Elser attempted an assassination with explosives at the beer cellar on 8th November 1938 to end the reign of the »brown regime«. But the explosion happened too late. Hitler had already left the building. An honorary plaque today reminds of Elser's brave deed.

The retirement home and brewery have disappeared today. In 1985 the civic cultural centre opened and dominates the *Gasteig* now. The people of Munich still mock the uninviting, massive red brick building and call it »*Kulturvollzugsanstalt*« (cultural enforcement authority). Nevertheless, they have accepted the *Gasteig* despite of its appearance and it has become one of Germany's most visited cultural centres. S Rosenheimer Platz

62 French Quarter

Baron Carl von Eichthal knew all the tricks on how to make the best business deals: to receive the right insider tips at the right time and act immediately. As a member of the East Railway-Station Association, the wealthy banker knew long before the public about the plans for the new railway station in the east. Eichthal quickly bought massive areas of land between *Rosenheimer Platz*, *Wörthstraße* and *Orleansplatz* for a knocked-down price, which in the eyes of the owners were worthless. He raised a new residential development from the grounds in 1870. Narrow and cheap tenements with a poor basic structure made for the less wealthy customers. The new housing estate quickly became known as the *Franzosenviertel* (French Quarter) because its street names derived from battlegrounds of the victorious war against France in 1870/71. S Rosenheimer Platz

63 Kultfabrik

Admittedly, the area actually belongs to *Berg am Laim* but because of its proximity to the *Ostbahnhof* (east railway station) it is often regarded as part of *Haidhausen*. Once the location for potato processing, it is the party hot spot of Munich's nightlife today. The factories of the company Pfanni used to be situated there. After Pfanni left the premises the *Kunstpark Ost* opened in 1996. It contained the highest density per square metre of entertainment in Europe with almost 30 discos and clubs, concert halls, bars, food stalls and restaurants. The owners changed in 2003 and it has since then been called *Kultfabrik*. As before, there

are still over 25 clubs, bars and various different venue locations along with around 100 commercial tenants, numerous theatre halls, Europe's largest indoor climbing hall, an artificial city beach, artist studios, music rehearsal rooms and plenty of top-class graffiti …

Next to the *Kultfabrik* are the premises of the *Optimolwerke*, opened in 2003, with numerous nightclubs. However, the end seems to be near. It is anticipated that a new modern city district will be built in 2016, offering a bold mix for living, partying, sports, work and culture. Grafinger Straße 6 • U/S Ostbahnhof

Basics

Another city next to the city? Only divided by a river? That was meant to go wrong. So, the city of Munich swallowed up the neighbouring town *Vorstadt* (suburb) *Au* in 1854.

It was no wonder that a settlement would emerge on the opposite side of the river Isar after the foundation of Munich. One could not live closer to the city than that. Presumably, many residents of the Au made a living with fishing. The monarchs used the village as starting point for their hunting excursions to the surrounding areas. The numerous streams, mainly the *Auermühlbach*, attracted the industry to settle in the *Au*. Armourers, mills for paper, sawing, plaster, oil, polish and whetting as well as cloth mills, tanneries and spinning mills settled here too and everything was powered by water. Max II Joseph even installed a »Porcellan-Fabrique« in his *Palace Neudeck* in 1747. It became the originator of today's Nymphenburger porcelain factory.

The industry in the *Au* and Munich's growth forced more and more workers and traders to move closer to the city. Because they were too poor to buy their civil right in Munich, they settled down in the neighbouring suburb *Au* instead. The suburb already struggled to cope with the increase in population in reputation remained. The people of Munich feared the residents of the *Au* as it was rumoured that they caught the townspeople's pet dogs to fatten them up and eventually roast them. The conditions did not improve and gangs of yobs ruled the streets. However, the population pressure also meant that the *Au* was to receive a glorious church. The foundation for today's *Mariahilfkirche* was laid in 1831 after plans by Daniel Ohlmüller. It was the first neo-gothic church construction it Bavaria.

In 1854, the year of the incorporation to the city, 10,840 people lived in the *Vorstadt Au* and the boom continued. The steep hill between *Quell-* and *Hochstraße*, which is a recreational area today, once accommodated one dwelling after another.

Bizarrely, glamour and squalor were at close quarters in the *Au* because the district not only attracted work-seekers but also Munich's nobility. First was Konrad der Preisinger in 1401, who built himself a luxurious summer residence. Other Patricians followed since having a palace on the other side of the Isar had suddenly become trendy. Duke Wilhelm IV had a hunting and pleasure palace erected in the 16th century near *Neudeck*. At royal behest, monks from the Order of St. Francis of Paola settled down

Munich's east: Au (Vorstadt Au)

First mentioned 12th December 1340 as »Awe ze Gyesingen« **Meaning** »Awe« = »Au« = floodland near the village of Giesing **Incorporation** 1st October 1854

near *Neudeck* from 1627 and established their own brewery. Apart from the brewery *Paulanerbräu*, the *Au* also gained another major brewery: *Franziskanerbräu* relocated its production to the *Lilienberg* at the *Hochstraße* in 1841. The last buildings were removed from the premises in 1971 and today include a residential housing complex.

1600. Even the shabbiest barn was rented out. In order to acquire right of residence many young guys quickly married some of the local widows, no matter how old or ugly they were. Everyone built their small houses where and how they liked in between the maze of the narrow alleys. In 1801, the *Au* was divided into seven quarters, named after colours, to create more clarity. Wooden boards on house corners in corresponding colours were meant to provide better orientation. The city council already deliberated in 1724 to incorporate the *Au* mainly to have better control over this disreputable place. Escaped perpetrators, beggars and scallywags as well as prostitutes made up to the street scene.

In the 18th century the *Au* suffered mostly from the fact that it was located outside the protective city walls. Wars shook up the land; soldiers from all over Europe invaded the *Au* again and again through pillaging, looting and rape.

In 1818 the *Au* was finally raised to become a city, officially named: *Vorstadt Au*. However, its abysmal

The *Au* expanded to the south and east in the 19th century when the royal pleasure palaces were long part of the history. Instead of the worker dwellings cheap tenements were built. After the war the *Au* remained an ill famed »broken glass quarter«. This only changed at the end of the 1990s. Suddenly people discovered the run-down district with its winding alleys. Since then, luxurious renovations and elegant newly built houses have caused booming rental fees. Lastly, the announcement of the *Paulaner* brewery to relocate their business from the *Au* caused shock among the residents because the locals fear that the premises will be used for Munich's typical upmarket housing developments.

64 Auer Dult

In 1796 Elector Karl Theodor granted the residents of the *Au* the right to host a fair twice a year and the so-called *Auer Dult* (Auer Fair) was born. The third and oldest fair, the *Jacobidult*, took place for the first time in Munich in 1310 at today's *St. Jakobs-Platz*. It was relocated at the end of the 18th century to the *Kaufinger-* and *Neuhauserstraße* and changed its location a few more times until it was also moved to the *Au*. Since 1905, three fairs take place every year at the *Mariahilfplatz*: the *Maidult* (May fair) at the end of May, the *Jacobidult* at the end of June and the *Kirchweihdult* (kermis fair) in October. Originally, the *dult* was a kind of trade fair but is now considered to be not only Europe's largest pottery fair but also offers many flea markets and antique stalls as well as a fun fair with nostalgic fun rides, beer gardens and numerous food stalls. The three fairs attract, as cosy little sister-fairs of the *Oktoberfest*, around 300,000 visitors every year. Mariahilfplatz • **U** Fraunhoferstraße or Kolumbusplatz • **Tram 17** Ohlmüllerstraße

Basics

Giesing suffered a conceivably bad reputation until a few years ago. It used to be a workers district with dirty windows, a bit like the Cinderella of towns beyond the Isar, which the citizens of Munich largely avoided. Nevertheless, Giesing held a strong tradition as one of the largest villages in the surrounding area of Munich and was first mentioned in 790, therefore is much older than Munich. Munich's oldest mill was located in Giesing and its wheels had already been working at the stream Auermühlbach since the 7th century. It was in use until 1972 and then demolished.

The farming village Giesing was early on strongly influenced by the densely populated district Au. The children of Giesing had to go to school in the Au. Even the cemetery, today's Ostfriedhof (East Cemetery), had to be shared. The reputation of Giesing started to suffer very early on due to the local madhouse, which opened in 1692 at the Kolumbusplatz. In vernacular terms, Giesing became synonymous for »madhouse«.

The transformation of the old Giesing from the famers village to the suburb of the city happened shortly after 1818. For centuries the village had almost steadily consisted of 20 working farms. From there on Giesing had grown rapidly. Like in the Au

sing experienced a heavy phase of construction with housing societies lifting entire new districts off the ground. An American settlement for the family members of the US-forces formed at the edge of the Perlacher Forst – the Americans also introduced Germany's first McDonald's restaurant in Giesing.

Some parts of Giesing experienced a massive upturn as attractive residential area in the last years. Particularly, the area comprising of many historic buildings between the East Cemetery and the underground station Silberhornstraße has been made up – often renovated to a luxurious standard – and attracts young and well-earning people. Untergiesing, mainly the area around Kolumbusplatz is becoming more and more the trendy district, not least because of its proximity to the Isar.

An important identification marking of Giesing is the football – after all, »Kaiser« Franz Beckenbauer also hails from Giesing. Above all, an important element of the district are the so-called Sechzger, the »Lions« of the football club TSV 1860 München. The stadium of the Sechzger, which was built between 1911 and 1926, is enthroned diagonally across from the Wettersteinplatz. Since 1945, the FC Bayern München has its home in the Säbener Straße just around the corner.

Munich's east: Giesing

First mentioned 14th July 790 as »Kyesinga«
Meaning settlement of a man called Kyso **Incorporated** 1st October 1854

and Haidhausen, more and more workers squeezed into the miserable workers settlements by the Isar hillside. After the incorporation in 1854, the district downright extended: 25,218 people lived here in 1900. Multi-storey apartment buildings for workers were constructed. Giesing offered the lowest rents in Munich and was regarded as one of the poorest boroughs.

The end for the historic town centre came in 1934: the old farms had to make way for a radial road. Only the farm Hauserbauernhof in the Silberhornstraße 2 still remains today at the busy junction between Heiligkreuzkirche and Martin-Luther-Kirche. It was Giesing's last working farm, which stopped its agricultural production in 1954.

Because the main population were workers and labourers, the district Giesing remained »red« and was a stronghold for communists and social democrats much to the dismay of the rising National Socialists. The citizens of Giesing often teamed up to give the »brown mob« a good beating and to get them off their streets. After the Second World War, Gie-

65 **Feldmüllersiedlung** (Feldmueller settlement)

Day-labourers did not fit into the old farmer village *Giesing*. They should build their cheap dwellings down by the Isar hillside. But Theres Feldmüller was plagued with financial worries. She had divorced her husband and with her father's inheritance bought a farm in *Giesing* where she maintained a small dairy business. Whenever she needed money, she sold parts of her grounds behind the parish church *Heilig-Kreuz* to day-labourers and tradesmen. As a result, the small settlement *Feldmüllersiedlung* with its small houses and tiny gardens evolved between 1840 and 1846. This collection of tiny houses still exists in large parts today. Because of its insight into the poor people's housing areas of the 19th century, it is considered to be important far beyond Munich's border for urban and social-historic reasons. The *Feldmüllersiedlung* differs from the unruly-built workers dwellings in the *Lohe*, *Au* and *Haidhausen* because its streets were systematically laid out. **U** Silberhornstraße

66 Heilig-Kreuz-Kirche (Holy Cross Church)

For two years two churches stood next to each other at the hill *Giesinger Berg*, as shown on the historic postcard: the small, old village church from the 12th century and the newly-built, large neo-gothic church *Heilig-Kreuz-Kirche*. Due to the heavy increase in population in *Giesing*, the old church had become too small. The new church was consecrated in 1886 and the old church was demolished two years later. A school is situated in its place today. The *Heilig-Kreuz-Kirche* was not destroyed during the Second World War and is therefore today Munich's only and completely preserved neo-gothic church. Gietlstraße 2

• U Silberhornstraße

67 Little Venice

One can hardly picture it today but Munich was once criss-crossed by numerous city streams. Most of those streams were drained at the end of the 1960s as part of the underground construction. What many areas of Munich might have looked like can be seen at the *Mondstraße*. It looks like a very small version of Venice but situated by the stream *Auermühlbach*.

Mondstraße • **U** Kolumbusplatz

68 Rosengarten (Rose Garden)

The official name of the site is »*Baumschule Bischweiler*« but everyone just calls it *Rosengarten* (Rose Garden). The public park was once a tree nursery founded in 1901. Today, it belongs to the horticultural department, which since 1955 has been testing which species of roses are suitable for inner-city cultivation. The site contains around 8,500 rose trees. Wall charts offer explanations. There are also themed gardens such as the poisonous plants garden, a touch and feel garden, a scent garden and the lilac garden. Sachsenstraße 2 • **U** Kolumbusplatz • summer: 7.00–21.00 • winter: 9.00–18.00

69 Archiconvent der Templer (Monastery of the Order of the Templar)

13 monks and 13 nuns (symbolic for Jesus and his disciples) lived and worked at the convent by the rules of the historic Order of the Knights Templar. In 1968, the order acquired a villa at *Birkeneiten* in *Untergiesing*. The jeweller Karl Winterthaler had the villa erected in 1880. The order reconstructed the building to a convent. The extraordinary 87m high, onion-shaped tower and its four smaller neighbour towers can been seen from afar. The *Archiconvent der Templer* was founded in 1932 and is dedicated mainly to the work with the poor and indigent. Birkenleiten 35 • **U** Candid-platz • not open to the public

70 Tierpark Hellabrunn

Originally, *Hellabrunn* was part of the property *Harlaching* and changed owner numerous times. For many years, the site contained only a farm and a mill from the 14th century. The old mill was dismantled in 1902. After long debates the city decided to buy the grounds and left it to the *Verein Zoologischer Garten München e. V.* The zoo, designed by Emanuel von Seidl opened its doors in 1911. The elephant house in the byzantine style is still the zoo's landmark. The First World War and the inflation prevented a further extension. The zoo even had to close in 1922. The park however, surprised its visitors during the reopening in 1928 with a revolutionary concept: *Hellabrunn* was the first geo-zoo in the world in which animals were classified by its geographical origin and shown in generous outdoor areas. Today, *Hellabrunn* offers around 7,700 species of animals and is known for its preservation of endangered species as well as the back breeding of extinct animals such as the Tarpan and Heck cattle. Tierparkstraße 30 • **U** Thalkirchen • summer: 9.00–18.00 • winter: 9.00–17.00

Basics

According to the findings of ancient graves, tribes had already settled at today's *Plinganserstraße* in 2000 BC. Probably around 600 AD, a tribe leader called Sendilo settled down here with his tribe and thereby gave the place its name. The noble dynasty Sentlinger, whose coat of arms includes a golden unicorn, established themselves in the village in the 12th century. The line of the Sentlinger dynasty ended at the end of the 16th century.

The village, drawn along the road from south to north, was very early own divided into three areas: *Unter-*, *Mitter-* and *Obersendling*. Various convents acted as landlords. After the terrors of the Thirty-Year-War, the convents were forced to sell parts of their possessions to financially strong aristocrats, who set up various noble domiciles, among them the *Sendling* Residence and the *Löwenhof*. Today there are no traces left of the *Sendling* Residence: the former compound of the palace has been replaced by the ring road *Mittlerer Ring*. The *Löwenhof*, however, is still present in some form. Part of the *Löwenhof* is a tavern, which Robert Harras acquired in 1869. The palace had to be demolished for a new-built, multi-storey apartment building in 1903 and the *Café Harras* reopened in the basement. Because of

hand rich city people built elegant villas along the slope of the Isar. In 1877, Munich swallowed up *Unter-* and *Mittersendling*. Despite the increasing urbanisation, mainly at the *Harras* and in the *Plinganserstraße*, the increase in population kept itself within a limit. Only 5,805 people lived there in 1908. This was the fault of the farmers of *Sendling*, who firmly refused to sell their cropland to construction companies. They feared that more industrial businesses would appear with smoking chimneys.

Because they were unwanted, the factories moved down south towards *Obersendling*. In 1927, the company, which still defines *Obersendling*, emerged: Siemens opened a branch and operated one of their largest facilities there. The National Socialists found it difficult to gain ground after the First World War in a »red« workers district like *Sendling*. Traditionally, one voted for the SPD (Social Democratic Party of Germany). However, after the shift in power, the people of *Sendling* had to conform to new times. The concentration camp *Dachau* set up two external camps in *Sendling*, whose inmates had to graft as forced labourers at the industrial sites.

After the war, *Sendling* experienced an enormous boost. Two thirds of all buildings formed after 1945.

Munich's west: Sendling

First mentioned 782 as »Sentilinga« **Meaning** settlement of a man called Sendilo **Incorporation** Unter-/Mittersendling: 1st January 1877; Obersendling: 1st January 1900

its central location at an important traffic interchange, the *Café Harras* provided the name for the entire traffic junction. Today, the *Harras* is one of Munich's most famous places.

Industry settled down with the construction of the railway. Numerous machine, motor and tobacco factories, such as the locomotive factory Krauß set up large production sites. The city of Munich built eleven large warehouses for grain, pulses, malt and seeds between 1871 and 1888 near the railway tracks. *Sendling* enjoyed a considerable boom when the city converted its grain halls in *Untersendling* to a warehouse modelled on Parisian examples. The *Großmarkthalle,* the »Belly of Munich«, which opened in 1912, is today one of the largest wholesale facilities in Europe. *Untersendling* serves a region with around 5 million people.

At time of the industrialisation, the three villages of *Sendling* lost their farming appearance. Residential areas started to expand. On one hand, tenements for the numerous labourers emerged and on the other

Siemens also played a considerate part in the rapid upturn. The concern relocated its seat from Berlin to Munich and the factory at the *Obersendlinger Hofmannstraße* became the central headquarter making the striking Siemens-high rise building a landmark of the area. The plans to replace the high-rise building with two individual buildings as one unity caused an extremely emotional petition for referendum in 2004. Since then, no construction in Munich can be built higher than the two towers of the *Frauenkirche*. Now, parts of the former Siemens sites are developed into trendy residential estates.

With some exceptions, *Sendling* is mainly a residential area today. But do not be fooled by the many faceless post-war apartment blocks. Particularly in the back roads between *Mittersendling* and *Waldfriedhof* stand grand villas with large gardens. The lowlands between *Lindwurmstraße* and *Großmarkthalle* became more and more popular and by now are regarded as a trendy district with its high share of historic buildings and the picturesque *Gotzinger Platz*. As a result, *Untersendling* suffers the typical consequences of gentrification and rental and property prices have rocketed.

71 Sendlinger Mordweihnacht (Sendling's Night of Murder)

The scent of blood lay heavily in the air at Christmas 1705. Elector Max Emanuel had supported the wrong side in the War of the Spanish Succession and had to go into exile to France. Munich was occupied by the troops of the Emperor Leopold I. He had increased taxes to such an extent, that there was widespread poverty throughout the land with subsequent revolts and rebellion. Munich was supposed to be liberated at Christmas. 2,769 rebels from the uplands marched onto the capital. On the night of 25th December the first of the bloody battles between farmers and royal troops commenced in the suburb of Isarvorstadt but the farmers lost. In a wild panic, they fled to *Untersendling* where they had set up their headquarters. Although many wanted to surrender or attempted to save themselves by hiding inside St. Margaret church, the Habsburger troops knew no mercy and proceeded to inflict an unimaginable bloodbath upon the farmers, destroying the gothic church as they went. Over 1,000 farmers died. The slaughter entered into the history books as the *»Sendlinger Mordweihnacht«*. The legendary blacksmith von Kochel, the alleged leader of the rebels is however not historically validated. Nevertheless, he has been honoured with a monument in the *Lindwurmstraße*.

Lindwurmstraße • **U** Harras or Implerstraße

72 Westpark

The Nazis attempted to erect a *Kraft-durch-Freude-Stadt* (Strength through Joy town) in an area of roughly 60 hectares of wasteland – living accommodations for the masses. This never happened. Instead, the *Internationale Gartenbauaustellung* (International Garden Show) was built there in 1983. Since the end of the garden show, the park is free for all visitors. A few of the attractions, which were meant to be dismantled after the event, were left in their original state. Among them the popular Nepalese Pagoda, which was carved in Nepal and used during its transport to Munich to smuggle around 400kg of cannabis within its cavities. Here every October the Hindu community perform their Festival of Light, whilst the Buddhist community celebrate their Full and New Moon rites. Of equally religious value is the Thai Sala and its sacred Buddha statue – the first holy Buddha sanctuary in Europe, where every May the Vesakh festival takes place. **U** Westpark

73 Flaucher

Bathing naked by the gravel banks, grilling sausage on the barbeque, to sit on a summer's night with beer by the banks of the Isar, listening to the gurgling of the water and the rustle of the trees …The *Flaucher* is one of the most beautiful local recreation areas in Munich and »local« is an apt description, as it is situated right in the centre of the capital. Unlike the other inner-city parks, the *Flaucher* conveys a far greater nature experience, even though achieved entirely by trickery: here the Isar is by no means wild and naturally winding anymore, but re-cultivated. On beautiful summers' days and mild evenings half of Munich will find their way to the gravel banks, islands and meadows of the *Flaucher*, situated between the power plant by the *Brudermühlbrücke* and *Thalkirchen*. The unusual name is the legacy of a local innkeeper, Johann Flaucher. He decided to change a hunter's lodge from about 1800 into an inn, which opened its doors in 1873, now named *»Zum Flaucher«*, which even today is a much-loved beer garden.

U Brudermühlstraße • Flaucher-Biergarten: Isarauen 8 (opening at 11.00)

Basics

Munich's smallest suburb, *Schwanthalerhöhe*, also popularly called *Westend*, does not have a long history. There was no village, convents did not have sinecures – nothing happened at the hill west of the city until the 19th century. Only a desolate tollhouse stood at the road towards *Pasing*, where customs duties were charged to passing carriages. The fields were barren and provided the farmers of *Sendling* with almost no earnings. The more profitable business proved to be the gravel trade, which the people of *Sendling* sold to Munich for construction purposes. In 1760, a small farmer tried his luck and bought a small house on the hillside.

The citizens of Munich only flocked to the *Schwanthalerhöhe* because the gallows used to be on the hill near today's *Hackerbrücke*. Munich's breweries discovered the area in the middle of the 18th century. They built storage houses for hops and barley. Later, they built up to 12m deep cellars to store and keep the beer chilled. In addition to keep the cellars cool, shady chestnut trees were planted above the cellars. When in 1812 serving beer in the beer cellars was permitted; visitors arrived in droves at the shady beer gardens at the *Schwanthalerhöhe*. The shooting stand was relocated to the *Theresien-*

rubber factory and various paint factories. A disgusting smell drifted through the alleys.

The housing shortage in the *Westend* remained tense despite enormous construction measures. The *Schwanthalerhöhe* remained the same after the war: a simple workers district with a very modest quality of living. Those who could afford to would move away. The apartments were rented cheaply to migrant workers. Until today, the *Westend* has one of the highest shares of foreign nationalities of all Munich boroughs. A comparable density of oriental shops can only still be found in the *Ludwigsvorstadt*. Naturally, the gentrification does not stop at the *Westend*. At the end of the 1990s, many young people, often with a creative profession, moved here because of the low rents. Since then, the district is intermittently appointed to be Munich's new artist quarter or trendy neighbourhood. Compared to other new trendy districts, the *Westend* has managed (so far) to retain its flair and mixed social structure and not to become a playing field for property speculators.

Munich's west: Schwanthalerhöhe (Westend)

First mentioned 4th December 1873 **Meaning** named after the sculptor Ludwig Schwanthaler, who created the monumental statue of Bavaria **Incorporation** 1st January 1877

höhe in 1852 when it had to make way for a new construction of the railway station outside the *Neuhauser Tor*.

Settlers were drawn to the area because of its breweries, the railway and the increasing business of sand digging in the large sand and gravel pits. In 1857, the brewery *Augustinerbräu* bought a storage cellar in the *Landsberger Straße* and relocated later its entire production site to the still existing premises. The breweries attracted large numbers of seasonal workers. Due to the inadequate cooling methods, the brewing of beer was purely seasonal work and it was not permitted to brew beer during the summer months. Hundreds of workers lived in the large beer factories, meaning, they worked and slept there. The increase in population quickly led to a dense development of multi-storey tenements and caused land speculations. Further industrial plants settled down, especially noise and odour intense companies, e.g. plants producing sulphuric, tar, vinegar as well as a

74 Bavaria

This was a world's first: Bavaria at the edge of the slope above the *Theresien-wiese* was the first colossal statue since antiquity entirely cast from bronze. It was and is to this day a marvel of technology, cast within the royal ore foundry in the *Maxvorstadt*. The sculptor Ludwig Schwanthaler designed the 18.52m tall allegory of Bavaria. Directly behind is the *Ruhmeshalle*, built by Leo von Klenze between 1843 and 1853. The three-winged Doric column hall was developed by request of King Ludwig I. Here all the distinguished personalities from all parts of Bavaria receive their honours, among them the playwright Berthold Brecht and the composer Carl Orff. Theresienhöhe 16 • **U** Theresienwiese • April–October: daily 9.00–18.00

75 Die endlose Treppe (The endless staircase)

One has to look twice: yes, on this staircase you can walk up and down without having to change direction. The endless staircase by the Danish/Icelandic artist Olafur Eiasson is officially called »*Um-schreibung*« (Paraphrase). Since 2004 it is situated in front of the headquarters of KPMG. Ganghoferstraße 29 • **U** Schwanthalerhöhe

76 Sweet Brown Snail

This is an ironic comment aimed at the *Verkehrszentrum* (Traffic Centre) right opposite: whilst dreams of speed are woven inside the walls of the museum, this cheerful snail stands happily for a somewhat slower pace. The artists Jason Thoades and Paul McCarthy designed the roughly 4m tall sculpture in 2002, mimicking a kitsch clay snail from a souvenir shop.

Theresienhöhe • **U** Schwanthalerhöhe

77 Verkehrszentrum (Traffic Centre)

Because the *Deutsches Museum* on the Museums' Island had long outgrown its space, additional venues had to be found. Thus since 2003, the *Verkehrszentrum* finds itself in 3 historic listed exhibition halls on the *Theresienhöhe*. All sorts of vehicles, from the automobile and train engines to bicycles and trams can be found around an area of about 12,000 square metres. The 3 halls are divided into the following themes: urban traffic (hall 1), journeys (hall 2), mobility and technology (hall 3). Am Bavariapark 5 • **U** Schwanthalerhöhe • daily 9.00–17.00

Basics

He arrived on a mule, originally on his way to the Holy Land and then got stuck in *Neuhausen*. Legend has it that a supposedly English itinerant preacher called Winthir brought Christendom to *Neuhausen* in the 8th century. As long as Winthir lived, *Neuhausen* was spared from pestilence and any kind of misfortune.

Reliable evidence of small towns in the area only emerged in 1025 when the village *Gern* is mentioned: the oldest settlement in the borough. One of the reasons why *Neuhausen* suddenly came into the spotlight in 1164 was the foundation of Munich in 1158. The important salt route now ran right through the village

Neuhausen changed very little through the centuries. The number of farms and inhabitants remained relatively steady. Until the marauding Swedish soldiers completely destroyed *Neuhausen* during the Thirty-Year-War.

In 1663, Elector Ferdinand Maria purchased the village *Kemnaten* northeast of *Neuhausen* for a cheap price, which after all, consisted of 28 working farms. He gave it to his wife Adelheid von Savoyen as a gift. The Electoral Princess had a palace built which she called *Nymphenburg*. *Kenmaten* became »royal

1846 and had it demolished. In its place large breweries set up and a stretch of barracks and military facilities emerged.

Within 30 years, *Neuhausen* experienced a downright explosion in population: when in 1855 only 683 people lived in the area, it had increased to 9,648 by 1885. The tram had already connected the village with the city for a while, property speculators discovered the area as playground and industry and military expanded. In 1800, the Bavarian capital absorbed *Neuhausen* and nine years later the villages *Nymphenburg* and *Gern* followed. In contrast to the noble *Nymphenburg* and the upper class *Gern*, *Neuhausen* was made up mainly from apartment blocks and workers accommodations but also important social facilities such as schools, hospitals and children's homes.

In 1903, the *Rotkreuzplatz* near the old *Neuhauser* hunting palace was set up as the districts centre point. Directly next to it formed the hospital *Rotkreuz-Krankenhaus*. The hospital and the palace were completely destroyed during the war. The hospital high-rise derives from the year 1967. Generally, the centre point in *Neuhausen* is mainly shaped by postwar architecture. Most striking and also controversi-

Munich's west: Neuhausen (Nymphenburg, Gern)

First mentioned around 1164 as »Niwenhusen« **Meaning** »neue Behausung« = new houses **Incorporation** 1st January 1890

village« and its original name disappeared because everyone called it *Nymphenburg*. Ferdinand Maria had a royal house in *Neuhausen* converted to conduct his favourite hobby: hunting. He hosted lavish par force hunts for his illustrious guests in the wide forests surrounding the village.

Neuhausen experienced the second largest catastrophe after the Thirty-Year-War in 1794 when a disastrous fire destroyed the old centre. The *Dorfstraße* was straightened out during the reconstruction and the farms, which used to be scattered around the village, were built to run along the road. The city slowly started to grow closer to *Neuhausen* in the 19th century. Rough settlements for day labourers emerged in the area between the *Maxvorstadt* and *Neuhausen*, whose inhabitants worked in the nearby gravel and sand pits, breweries or railway constructions. Disastrous conditions reigned at the settlements, just like at the workers dwellings in *Haidhausen*, *Giesing* or *Au*. Scallywags and criminals roamed through the dirty alleys. The people of *Neuhausen* welcomed it therefore when Munich incorporated the slum in

al construction is the current department store *Kaufhof* from the late 1970s. *Neuhausen* developed in the 1980s thanks to its quiet streets and high number of historic buildings to a popular residential area among students and young families, offering lots of trendy bars and alternative shops. During the past years, the gentrification also had an impact in *Neuhausen*. The rental and property prices have risen. Particularly, the picturesque and historic terraced houses in *Gern* are highly desired and by now almost unaffordable.

78 Herz-Jesu-Kirche (Sacred Heart of Jesus Church)

That modern architecture can be a magnet for visitors is proven by the new *Herz-Jesu-Kirche* in *Neuhausen*. Originally this church was simply an altered gymnasium from 1890, which was destroyed in the Second World War. The replacement building from the 1950s burned to the ground on 28th November 1994. The spectacular new glass cube, inaugurated in 2000, was the brainchild of the Munich architects Allmann Sattler Wappner. On special religious holidays the entire front opens like an enormous two-winged gate. Lachnerstraße 8 • **U** Rotkreuzplatz

79 Hubertusbrunnen

At the eastern end of the Nymphenburger canal resides the fountain *Hubertus-brunnen*. Adolf von Hildebrand created the fountain, finished in 1907, in the form of a temple. Originally it stood in front of the Bavarian National Museum in the *Prinzregetenstraße*. It was dismantled in 1937 and only in 1954 re-erected in its current location. Waisenhausstraße • **U** Gern

80 Nymphenburg

The Elector was mighty happy: his wife Henriette Adelaide von Savoyen had, in the year of 1662, finally given birth to his son and heir Max Emanuel. Elector Ferdinand Maria was so delighted that in his enthusiasm he bequeathed an entire village to his wife as a weekend retreat. This village was called *Kemnaten* and the Electoral Princess had great plans. In 1664 she had a palace built called »Borgo delle Ninfe«. The architect Agostino Barelly designed the palace in the style of a 5-story Italian country house with double-winged floating staircases on either side. In 1665 the Electoral Princess moved in and in the following centuries the building underwent numerous alterations and extensions. Max Emanuel proved to be especially keen on building further additions as between 1728 and 1758 the bastion saw the erection of 10 palaces for important court employees. In 1761 the court porcelain manufacturers moved from *Palace Neudeck in der Au* to *Nymphenburg*.

Originally there was only a tiny garden in the Italian style attached to the building, which was remodelled into a French Baroque-style park at the beginning of the 18th century. The current generous country park, modelled on the English style, originated between 1804 and 1823.

Palace Nymphenburg served as summer residence for the Bavarian rulers and even today enjoys the patronage of the current head of the House of Wittelsbach, Duke Franz von Bayern, although since 1918 the palace is the property of the Bavarian state. The Botanical Gardens were and are not actually part of the palace complex.

By the way, the great fountain in front of the *Palace Nymphenburg* is operated by a pumping mechanism from 1807. It is, even today, in its original condition and most definitely the oldest operational machine in Europe, possibly even the world. Schloss Nymphenburg 1 • **Bus** 51/**Tram** 17 • summer: 9.00–18.00, winter: 10.00–16.00

81 Blutenburg

A mansion and a chapel surrounded by a moat – that is how the ancient weir system from the 12th century must once have appeared to the spectator. Only since Duke Albrecht III has reliable proof been found about the history of *Blutenburg*. Albrecht fell head-over-heels in love with Agnes Bernauer from Augsburg, the daugther of a barber surgeon, and had *Blutenburg* remodelled and enlarged as a Love Nest – a scandalous arrangement! The court was in uproar! Happiness for the couple lasted only until 1435, when Albrecht's father, Duke Ernst, had Anges arrested in Straubing and drowned in the Danube. Later on Albrecht's son Sigismund lived in *Blutenburg* and founded the still beautifully preserved late gothic palace chapel.

After many ownership-changes the palace was finally leased to the Sisters of Loreto in 1866. In 1957 the Sisters of the Third Order of the Nymphenburger Hospital took on the palace and opened an old people's home, which existed until 1976. Afterwards, a sensible plan had to be devised for its use and comprehensive renovation works began. Since 1983 the *Blutenburg* serves as the headquarters of the International Youth Library.

The death march of the concentration camp victims of Dachau led directly past the castle, which is commemorated by a monument by the sculptor Hubertus von Pilgrim. Seldweg 15 • **Bus** 56, 143, 160 • chapel: 10.00–16.00

Basics

Almost no other district of Munich is as well known in the world as *Schwabing*. Welcome to the district, which is, as generally known, a state of mind rather than a place. But even that state of mind once started as a small place, presumably as bajuwaren settlement. *Schwabing* officially emerged in the year 782. Soon the »*Herren von Schwabing*« appeared, who came from an aristocratic dynasty whose line ended in the 14th century. The »*Herren von Schwabing*« resided in the small castle (between *Haimhauser-*, *Occam-* and *Gohrenstraße*), also belonging to their village was a mill at the stream *Schwabinger Bach* as well as various farms. *Schwabing* remained a small locality for centuries. Munich built a leper's house far outside from the city walls in 1467 on the border to *Schwabing* (corner of *Leopold-/Nikolaistraße*) because pestilence and famine shook the country. Later, the rich people of Munich discovered the village in the north and bought themselves country estates. Palaces such as *Suresnes*, *Biederstein* and the *Gohrenschlössl* came into existence.

In the 18th century Munich slowly but surely grew closer to *Schwabing*. Initially, only in the form of the English Garden but from thereon, Munich townspeople would stroll on a Sunday away from the *Stephanie* and the Art Academy. Munich was regarded as the art capital in those years. Students and artists did not distinguish between living, working and partying on this side or the other side of the *Georgenstraße*, thus either in *Schwabing* or *Maxvorstadt*. *Schwabing* was synonymous with bubbling creativity, comparable with Montmartre in Paris. In contrast to the ultra-conservative city Berlin, one could live and work freely in Munich. Wladimir Iljitsch Lenin settled down in the *Kaiserstraße* in 1900. Wassily Kandinsky developed the abstract painting. Thomas Mann, August Macke, Rainer Maria Rilke, Giorgio de Chirico, Paul Klee, Lovis Corinth – only to name the most famous – worked here. Even Picasso envied the people of *Schwabing*. *Schwabing* was hip. The increasingly dense population rapidly extended the district. In 1909, *Schwabing* had already expanded so far towards the west that a new borough had to be created: *Schwabing-West*.

The political climate changed suddenly with the end of the First World War. Munich became ultra-conservative and the bohemian lifestyle came to an end. Almost half of the houses in *Schwabing* fell victim to the bombs in the Second World War, which is why many streets of the quarter are shaped by faceless

Munich's north: Schwabing

First mentioned 782 as »Suuapinga« **Meaning** from »Swapo« = Schwabe ≠ settlement of a Swabian person **Incorporation** 20th November 1890

narrow alleys of the city through the English Garden towards *Schwabing* only to quench their thirst and replenish at the popular inns for the way back home.

In 1880, *Schwabing* already counted over 5,000 inhabitants and was appointed city status seven years later. The young city soon struggled with the duties but most of all with the expenses. Things were not done by half. In 1889, *Schwabing* treated itself to the luxury of electric street lightning even before Munich, which still used gas to illuminate the streets. The mountain of debts grew. Not even four years later the city of *Schwabing* begged Munich imploringly to incorporate them.

In 1890 the independence of *Schwabing* ended and Munich grew by another 11,589 citizens. In those years, the myth about Schwabing emerged – even if some of the die-hard »*Schwabinger*« had to admit that some of those fundamental places of that myth were not located in *Schwabing* but in *Maxvorstadt*: the university, the artist bar *Simplicissimus*, the café

post-war architecture today. Shortly after the war, things started to heat up again in *Schwabing* and the nightlife club scene established itself. Hippies, beatniks and communards were part of the street scene in the 1960s and 1970s. Jimi Hendrix trashed his first guitar at the »Big Apple«.

But the great time ended with the 1980s. The »most beautiful daughter of Munich« mutated into a »Grande Dame«. The gentrification with luxurious renovations and rocketing rental fees caught *Schwabing* first out of all Munich's districts. All that was left was the name, which mostly property companies furthermore exploited. For decades, *Schwabing* has frequently been called dead. The dazzling bars at the *Feilitzschplatz* and along the *Leopoldstraße* are regarded among most people as total tourist traps but every year thousands of tourists stroll through the romantic streets of *Alt-Schwabing* and the English Garden attracts millions of visitors ever year. How does the saying go: »There is life in the old dog yet.«

82 Elisabethmarkt

The heart of western Schwabing is the *Elisabethmarkt* at the *Elisabethplatz*. This is one of Munich's four permanent markets selling food and flowers (as well as the *Viktualienmarkt*, *Pasinger Viktualienmarkt* and *Wiener Markt*). The *Elisabethmarkt* has been held at its current site since 1903; however, it is the modern version of a much older market, which was situated at the *Maffeianger*. A popular meeting point is the little restaurant *»Wintergarten«* with its beer garden. Elisabethplatz • **U** Josephsplatz • mon–sat from 7.00

83 Walking Man

A white giant strides through *Schwabing*: 17m high is the fibreglass statue by the American artist Jonathan Borofsky and has stood since 1995 outside the headquarters of the Munich Re in the *Leoploldstraße*. Leopoldstraße 36 • **U** Giselastraße

84 St. Ursula

Because *Schwabing* expanded ever westwards towards the end of the 19th century, a new church was to be commissioned at the town centre. This idea never quite came to pass, but St. Ursula provides a distinctive sight at the end of the *Friedrichstraße*. Architect Friedrich von Thiersch's designs follow very clearly the Florentine Renaissance. The »Cathedral of Schwabing« was consecrated in 1897. The old village church of *Schwabing*, previously under the patronage of the St. Ursula, became St. Sylvester in 1921. Kaiserplatz 1 • **U** Münchner Freiheit

85 Münchner Freiheit

Originally this was called *Feilitzschplatz*, then, under the Nazis, *Danziger Freiheit*. Since 1946 it is called *Münchner Freiheit* (Freedom of Munich) in honour of the resistance group »*Freiheitsaktion Bayern*« (FAB – Bavarian Action for Freedom). Just before the end of the war in 1945, under their leader Rupprecht Gerngross, the FAB had appealed for capitulation before the approaching US troops and called for an armed hunt of NS-Bonzen. The Gestapo (Secret State Police) and the SS managed to capture 40 members of the FAB and executed them all. Gerngross managed to go into hiding. The fancy green and white tram station, developed by the Aachener Office »Ox2«, has defined the place since 2010. **U** Münchner Freiheit

86 Suresnes

It would seem the cabinet minister Franz von Wilhelm only held the best memories of his time in exile, which he spent at the Chateau de Suresnes near Paris with the Elector Max Emanuel. Back in Munich in 1718, he hired Johann Baptist Gunetzrhainer to build his *Palace Surenes* after the French original. In the 19th century the house, also known as *»Werneckschlössl«*, became a popular meeting point for artists. Paul Klee's studio was situated here in 1919. In 1937 the archdiocese Munich and Freising bought the palace as a day-centre for the Catholic Academy in Bavaria. Werneckstraße 24 • **U** Münchner Freiheit • not open to the public

87 Kleinhesseloher See (Kleinhesseloher Lake)

A parking attendant had the idea to build a provisory beer counter for workers directly next to the artificial pond in the English Garden. This provision became a permanent state and many a rambler came here to rest, whilst a dance floor enticed even more visitors. In 1812, the lake's size increased to its current dimensions and the beer counter became a proper beer garden. Today the *Seehaus* offers around 2,500 seats with a view to the lake and its rowing and pedal boats. Kleinhesselohe 3 • **U** Münchner Freiheit • daily 10.00–1.00

88 St. Sylvester

The tiny alleys around St. Sylvester make it still very evident that this once was the site of the old village square of *Schwabing*. Supposedly a church had already stood here by the 8th century. The oldest parts of the tower however are from the 12th century. The first documented reference of this church followed in 1315. In those days, John the Baptist was patron and St. Sylvester deputy patron of the church. In the 17th century expansion works were carried out and the church redecorated in the Baroque style, whilst it was now devoted to St. Ursula. St. Ursula moved 1897 to the new church in the *Kaiserplatz*, and the old church was consecrated to Sylvester in 1921. Seamlessly integrated in the same style of Baroque, an octagonal expansion to the north side of the church by the architect Hermann Bucherts was added between 1925/26. Biedersteiner Straße 1 • **U** Münchner Freiheit

Jugendstil

Art Noveau, the playful artistic style popular around the turn of the century is called »*Jugendstil*« in Germany. The name derives from the Munich newspaper »Jugend« (Youth), founded in 1896 and Munich was one of the most important centres of the *German Jugendstil*. Alongside eminent buildings like the *Prinzregententheather*, the *Kammerspiele* and the *Müllersche Volksbad* are also several residential houses in the *Jugendstil* style, which have survived the nighttime bombings of the Second World War. *Schwabing* especially has many delights for the enthusiast. Our examples on these pages can be found at: Ainmillerstraße 22, Franz-Joseph-Straße 19 (backside), Franz-Joseph-Straße 23, Franz-Joseph-Straße 38, Römerstraße 11 and Schellingstraße 24.

Basics

Milbertshofen developed from a small estate, which probably already existed around the year 1000, along an ancient Roman street. Despite many owner changes, the estate flourished. The Elector, later to be King Max I Joseph, searched for a buyer through a newspaper ad in 1799. Four farmer families from the Oberpfalz acquired the enormous grounds and thereby set up the village. More settlers joined and the small village turned into a city. On 1st May 1910, Milbertshofen was appointed the city status. Huge debts forced the city Milbertshofen to almost

Basics

Allianz-Arena, motorway exit, rubbish pit – not much else is there to say about Fröttmaning. In fact, apart from the small church there are no further traces of the historic village near Freimann, which was recorded for the first time in the year 815. That is when the church was consecrated. Which would make the Fröttmaninger church Heilig Kreuz the oldest in Munich unless St. Martin in Moosach (also recorded for the first time in 815) would not claim that title as well. Fröttmaning was a poor village. Droughts, floods and war made life for the

Munich's north: Milbertshofen

First mentioned between 1149 and 1152 as »Ilmungeshoven« **Meaning** farm of a man called Ilmung; the name changed through the ages to »Milberzhofen« (1468) **Incorporation** 1st April 1913

Munich's north: Fröttmaning

First mentioned 19th April 815 as »ad Freddamaringun« **Meaning** settlement of a man called Fridumar (= the Peaceful) **Incorporation** 30th January 1935

offer itself to Munich and Munich agreed to the incorporation in 1913. Milbertshofen developed to an important industrial location. The industrial family Petuel contributed largely to that with several companies. Later, the company Knorr-Bremse arrived – today the world's leading manufacturer of brake systems for commercial vehicles. Immediately next to it, the world famous company BMW formed from the Gustav-Otto-Flugwerk, which had been set up in 1916. The reason for aircraft companies to settle down in Milbertshofen was due to the adjoining area Oberwiesenfeld, a gravel field, which had served as airport since the end of 19th century. The industry brought Milbertshofen its dark chapter during the NS regime: Forced labour camps and the »Judensiedlung Milbertshofen« (Jewish settlement), where thousands of Munich Jews were held until their transport to the extermination camps.

Because of its strong industrial relevance, Milbertshofen was heavily destroyed during the Second World War. Today Milbertshofen offers two extremely popular tourist attractions with the Olympic Park and the world of BMW but the environment does not benefit from that. Huge apartment blocks, many of them council flats, shape the appearance of the district. No traces are left of the old village. Milbertshofen offers a high number of jobs through its industry and therefore also denotes a high share of foreign nationals. However, high unemployment and poverty also exist in the district.

farmers difficult. The barren soil of Munich's north provided little income. Particularly, shepherds took their flocks therefore to the meagre meadows. Sheep were still part of the townscape until the 20th century. Fröttmaning did not experience a boom like other villages and townspeople hardly made their way there. The beginning of the end came after the Second World War: Munich gradually bought the old farms to create space for the motorway junction München-Nord. At the end of the 1960s, the rest of Fröttmaning disappeared underneath the rubbish of the city's landfill Großlappen. Nothing remained apart from the old church, which derived from the 12/13th century in its current form. The reason it still exists is thanks to protests by the townspeople, who frequently saved it from destruction. Lastly, the construction of the Allianz-Arena jeopardised the house of prayer but Heilig Kreuz remained. Thanks to the football stadium, Fröttmaning is now world famous. The former rubbish tip is today a re-cultivated local recreation area. A replica of the church Heilig Kreuz, built partially into the hillside and a work of art by Timm Ulrichs, reminds of what is buried next to Munich's household rubbish: the historic settlement of Fröttmaning.

89 Ost-West-Friedenskirche (East West Church of Peace)

Munich's mayor called it the »most adorable illegal building in Munich«. The Russian refugee Timofei Wassiljewitsch Pochorow, known as *Väterchen Timofei*, proceeded after the war to build for himself a house out of the ruins and debris on the *Oberwiesenfeld*, including a kitchen and even a chapel. When the Olympic village was proposed to be built on the site and Timofei forcibly moved, a massive protest by the townspeople resulted in the old man and his life-partner Natascha being able to stay put. The Olympic village was moved to another site, and Timofei died in 2004 at the grand old age of 110. His abode can still be visited today. Spiridon-Louis Ring 100 • **U** Olympiapark • daily 10.00–16.00

90 BMW Welt

BMW belongs to Munich like beer or the *Frauenkirche*. At home in the north of Munich since 1916, the company is one of the biggest employers in the city. Already in 1973, with the recently finished administrative building, the *»Vierzylinder«*, BMW stood at the forefront of modern town planning. Alongside is the *BMW Museum*, which, due to its shape, the locals call the *»Salad Bowl«*. Even more astonishing to behold is the *BMW Welt*, opened in 2007 and designed after plans by the Coop Hilmmelb(l)au and Professor Prix. Originally designed purely as a despatch centre, it is now an adventure-, museum-, and event site around the brand of BMW and one of the great tourist attractions of Munich. Am Olympiapark 2 • **U** Olympiapark • daily 9.00–18.00

91 Olympiapark

Originally, this was the site of the *Oberwie-senfeld* airport. After its relocation to *Riem* the site lay neglected for a lengthy period. After the war it became a massive rubbish pit, filled with the debris and masonry of the destroyed buildings of Munich. Homeless people took shelter among the detritus and built tiny huts. The only ad hoc settler that managed to stay after the building work commenced was the Russian Väterchen Timofej. The old man enjoyed cult status (see page 151).

In 1966, after Munich got the funding to build the Olympic village, the architect offices of Behnish & Partner, together with the landscape architect Günther Grzimek, developed the layout of the prestigious sports and spa area. The entire costs came to 1.35 billion DM (around 657 million Euro). Especially striking are the tent-like roof designs by Frei Otto, which even today emit a futuristic appeal. The Olympic Tower at 291m, had already been built serving as a TV tower. Here, at 200m above ground, you will find the Rock Museum of Munich.

U Olympiapark

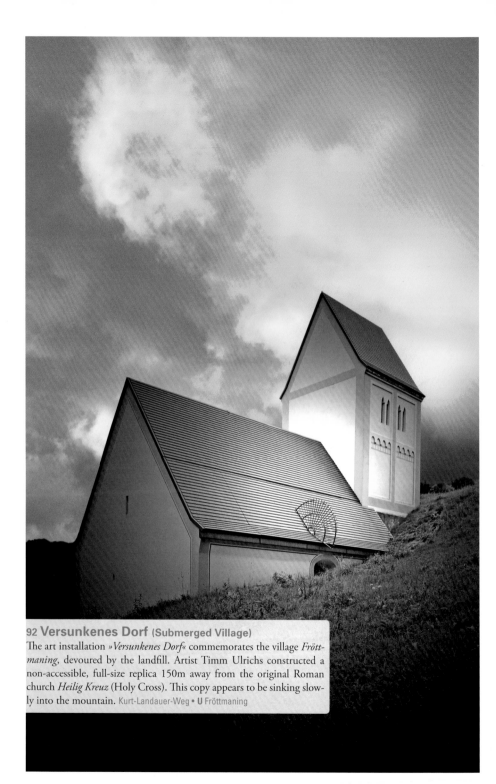

92 Versunkenes Dorf (Submerged Village)

The art installation »Versunkenes Dorf« commemorates the village Frött-maning, devoured by the landfill. Artist Timm Ulrichs constructed a non-accessible, full-size replica 150m away from the original Roman church Heilig Kreuz (Holy Cross). This copy appears to be sinking slow-ly into the mountain. Kurt-Landauer-Weg • U Fröttmaning

93 Allianz Arena

When the Allianz Arena is lit up in red or blue at night it looks like a gigantic UFO has landed next to the motorway. 1,056 foil pillows create the lighting effect. The Arena, opened in 2005 and designed by Herzog & de Meuron, has been developed from the beginning as a stadium exclusively for football. More than 71,000 people fit into the stadium. Both traditional Munich football clubs, FC Bayern München and TSV 1860 München, carry out their home games here. Moreover, it hosted various football games during the football world cup in 2006 and the UEFA Champions League final in 2012. The Arena originally belonged to both clubs; however, the FC Bayern has now bought all shares and is sole owner. Werner-Heisenberg-Allee 25 • **U** Fröttmaning

And finally: the beer

To brew beer in Munich? Not many thought of that in the 13th century. Sure, there were a few breweries but mostly the housewives would brew their own »beer« at home. Proper beer was imported at high costs from the north German city Einbeck! The brewers of Munich had wanted to set up their own guild but the Duke refused: it is not worth it! Wine was slowly pushed aside in the pubs after the royal brewery *Hofbräuhaus* had started to brew beer after »Einbeck« customs.

Almost 100 years earlier, on 23rd April 1516, Duke Wilhelm IV issued the Bavarian Purity Law based on the Munich Purity Law. The law dictated already since 1447 that only barley, hops and water were to be used for Munich beer. The purity law did not only dictate the taste. Henbane, deadly nightshade, labrador tea, opium poppy or vermouth – all those psychedelic substances had once been added. You would go on quite a trip drinking that beer. The Bavarian Purity Law also acts as a drugs law. Beer should not contain anything stronger than alcohol.

Munich beer was originally dark in colour. It was only allowed to be brewed in the winter because it started to moulder very quickly without refrigeration. The deep beer cellars with their shady chestnut trees on top produced a bit of relief. Their roots were flat and therefore did not destroy the cellar vaults. Beer lasted there for a couple of months. First it was strongly prohibited to serve beer from the storage cellars to private customers but nobody stuck to the rule. The era of the Bavarian beer gardens started when serving beer from the beer cellars officially became permitted in 1812. It was still not permitted to serve food; this service was still only reserved for the restaurants. Until today, it is allowed to bring your own food to a beer garden.

Dark beer is hardly being drunk anymore in Munich. The typical Munich beer is the *Helle* (light in colour), also known as *Export* or *Lager*. The large Munich breweries like *Augustiner, Spaten-Franziskaner, Hacker-Pschorr, Paulaner, Hofbräu* and *Löwenbräu* are the only breweries, which are approved for the *Oktoberfest*.

A very short city history

5.600 – 2.200 BC Stone-primeval settlements in *Laim*, *Pasing*, *Moosach* and *Sendling*

2.200 – 1.000 BC Bronze-primeval settlements in Munich's Old Town, *Harlaching*, *Grünwald* and at *Luitpoldpark*

Celtic era Square ditched enclosures in *Aubing*, *Langwied*, *Feldmoching* and *Perlach*

Roman era Roman settlements in *Aubing*, *Englschalking*, *Denning*, *Unterföhring* and *Grünwald*

Late Antiquity Traces of settlements at the *Petersbergl*

8th century Settlement of monks at the *Petersbergl*

1158 City founded by Henry the Lion and respectively first documented reference in the *Augsburger Schied* (charter)

1175 First city fortification

1180 Munich now belongs to the Bishop of Freising

1200 Ludwig der Kehlheimer is the first Bavarian Duke to verifiably enter Munich

1214 First documented reference of Munich town charter

1239 First appearance of the *Münchner Kindl* – on an official charter seal which relieves the township from bridge customs duties

1240 Munich is owned by the Wittelsbach dynasty instead of the bishops

1255 Munich becomes residence of the duchy *Oberbayern*

1271 Consecration of the *Frauenkirche* as second parish church

1285 Severe persecution of Jews

1328 The city is Imperial Residence for two years. It is extended and a second layer of city walls is constructed

1397–1402 Rebellion of the guilds against the Patricians and Wittelsbach dynasty

1442 Duke Albrecht III expels all Jews from Munich and the entire region of *Oberbayern*

1494 Consecration of the new *Frauenkirche*, built in 1468

1505 Munich becomes sole capital of Bavaria after the reunification of the duchies

1550–1579 Duke Albrecht V elevates Munich to a centre of Renaissance art

1623 Munich becomes ducal residence during the Thirty-Year-War

1632 The Swedish occupy Munich

1634 The plague rages in Munich and kills a third of the population

1657 Munich's first opera house opens

1704 The Habsburg dynasty occupies Munich during the War of the Spanish Succession. Sendling's Night of Murder happens one year later

1742 Occupation by the Habsburg dynasty during the War of the Austrian Succession

1789 Munich opens up: installation of the English Garden and the start of the demolition of the city walls

1806 Munich becomes capital of the new Kingdom of Bavaria

1825–1848 King Ludwig I elevates Munich to become a world-ranked city of art

1826 A new synagogue is consecrated again

1827 Foundation of the first protestant church in Munich

1839 The first train travels from Munich to Augsburg

1876 The first tram carries passengers

1886–1912 The city experiences a new cultural and technological boom under Prince Regent Luitpold, Munich »glows«

1899 The first worldwide driving test takes place in Munich and the first car number plate is issued

1901 Munich exceeds 500,000 citizens and is the third largest German city after Berlin and Hamburg

1907 The artistic group »*Der Blaue Reiter*« (Blue Rider) is founded

1918 Revolution and collapse of the monarchy, Bavaria becomes a free state (free from monarchy)

1919 Proclamation and downfall of the »*Räterepublik Baiern*« (Bavarian Soviet Republic)

1923 Hitler's Beer Hall Putsch fails

1935 Hitler appoints Munich to the »Capital of Movement«

1943 Thanks to the group »White Rose« and other brave opponents of the Nazi regime, Munich becomes the »Capital of Counter Movement«

1944/45 Severe destruction through bombs in the Second World War

1945 American troops liberate the city on 30th April

1957 For the first time, Munich counts over 1 million citizens

1971 Opening of the first pedestrian zone in Munich

1972 Olympic Games in Munich

1992 Opening of Munich's new airport

2005 Opening of the new Allianz-Arena football stadium

2005 Opening of the new Jewish community centre at the *St.-Jakobs-Platz*

Picture credits / Imprint

All current photos **Martin Arz**;
except page 95 a. l.: SWM/Robert Götzfried,
page 152/153: Interfoto/Gervasi and page 157:
Interfoto/imagebroker/Hermann Dobler
All historical photos **Hirschkäfer Verlag Archiv**
All maps © Hirschkäfer Verlag 2013

1st edition, October 2013

Idea, text and design: Martin Arz/Coriander P.
English translation: Tanja Jones, London
Print: Druckservice Brucker, Mainburg

ISBN978-3-940839-30-5

Visit us online:
www.hirschkaefer-verlag.de

Made with love.